THE

World's Greatest

DAD

DEVOTIONAL

BIBLE WISDOM FOR FATHERS

BARBOUR BOOKS
An Imprint of Barbour Publishing, Inc.

© 2017 by Barbour Publishing, Inc.

Compiled and edited by Jess MacCallum.

Print ISBN 978-1-68322-005-3

Published by Barbour Books, an imprint of Barbour Publishing, Inc., P.O. Box 719, Uhrichsville, Ohio 44683, www.barbourbooks.com

Our mission is to publish and distribute inspirational products offering exceptional value and biblical encouragement to the masses.

 Member of the
Evangelical Christian
Publishers Association

Printed in China.

*But the wisdom that comes from heaven is first of all pure;
then peace-loving, considerate, submissive,
full of mercy and good fruit, impartial and sincere.*

JAMES 3:17 NIV

Welcome to The World's Greatest Dad Devotional!

Here's to Dad: the man of the house, the best playmate, the guy with all the best (and worst) jokes, role model, and friend. Here's a collection of more than 200 devotions that are a great source of encouragement for dads of all ages. Bible wisdom and spiritual insight pack a powerful punch—the perfect fit for the world's greatest!

I can't remember when I became a son, but I sure remember the day I became a father! It was a milestone, a miracle and a mystery all wrapped up in a squalling little bundle. And it was the beginning of seeing God, the Father, in a whole new way.

When I began to seriously follow Jesus at sixteen, I poured myself into knowing Him. Spiritually, all my experiences were framed from a child's point of view—how to please my heavenly Father as an obedient son. When I got married at twenty-three, I began to experience things from a husband's point of view, sharing some of the emotions and desires Christ feels toward His bride, the Church. Then having our first child at twenty-seven, I started to gain a totally different perspective—that of a parent. All the ideas I had about being a dad prior to my son's birth fell flat compared to experiencing it for myself. I could (in some limited human way) relate to God not just as my Father, but as a *fellow* father. He and I had something in common that we didn't have before. In some mysterious way, I could sympathize and rejoice with Him! What an amazing gift He has granted to dads—and what an awesome responsibility.

I pray that these devotional readings will encourage you in your journey as a man and as a father, knowing that for all the tenderness and love and patience we have for our children, God has infinitely more for each of us.

Jess MacCallum, Editor

Your Father Is There for You

The righteous cry out, and the LORD hears them;
He delivers them from all their troubles.
PSALM 34:17 NIV

● ●

Those who have lived the Christian life for any length of time have likely had a good chance to learn an important lesson about a life of faith, namely that God never promised that it would be easy or that there wouldn't be times of difficulty.

Indeed, any effort to find a scriptural promise telling us that the Christian life is a trouble-free life would end in frustration and failure. In fact, Jesus promised quite the opposite when He said, "In this world you will have trouble. But take heart! I have overcome the world" (John 16:33 NIV).

Yes, in this world we're going to face times of trouble. But there is one promise God has made repeatedly in His written Word for believers facing times of difficulty. Time and time again, He tells us, "I'll be there for you."

God is our loving heavenly Father, who provides us with all we need to emerge from the difficult times as overcomers.

With a Father like Him, who needs. . .*anything else?*

Heavenly Father, we have been made righteous in Christ,
so we can cry out to You at any time, for any reason,
confident that You care for us as Your children. Help us
to imitate Your love and patience as fathers ourselves.

How Much Is "Enough"?

*Whoever loves money never has enough; whoever loves wealth
is never satisfied with their income. This too is meaningless.*
ECCLESIASTES 5:10 NIV

• •

The 1987 movie *Wall Street* contains an often-quoted line: "Greed, for lack of a better word, is good."

But the Bible warns that greed is not good, that greed is a destructive force in the life of any man—especially a man of God.

The apostle Paul wrote that "the love of money is a root of all kinds of evil" and that some who have an insatiable desire have "wandered from the faith and pierced themselves with many griefs" (1 Timothy 6:10 NIV).

God is not against earning money—even against accruing wealth—as long as we do it through righteous means and with righteous motivation. In fact, the Bible repeatedly encourages God's people to work hard so that they may prosper. What God is against—passionately against—is making money an idol, a life's focus ahead of family and, yes, ahead of God Himself.

Work is God's provision for men to provide well for themselves and their families, but never lose sight of the fact that your ultimate satisfaction, your ultimate source of all good things, is your heavenly Father.

*Father, Provider, we know all good things come from You, and we thank
You for providing for us and through us to the blessing of our families.*

God-Honoring Humility

Humble yourselves, therefore, under God's mighty hand,
that he may lift you up in due time.
1 PETER 5:6 NIV

• •

It's probably fair to say that pride is at the heart of nearly every sin we can commit against God and against others. Pride causes people to boast about themselves and to tear others down. Pride causes people to believe they can do for themselves what God has promised to do for them, and that leads to a lack of prayer. Pride causes conflicts between people, and it keeps us from confessing our sins to one another and to God so that we can be reconciled.

This list of the terrible results of human pride could go on and on, but when you read it, it is no small wonder that God has said, "I hate pride" (Proverbs 8:13 NIV).

God hates human pride, but He loves humility, which can be defined as the acknowledgment that apart from Him, we are nothing and can do nothing of value. When we are humble, in effect we are confessing that we have nothing to offer God apart from what He has already done.

Humbling yourself before God never ends badly. Wait patiently for your Father to lift you up in His timing.

Mighty God, our patient Father, we wait upon You, trusting
Your timing to lift us up when You think best. Help us to be wise
toward our own children, caring for them as You care for us.

Read Your Bible!

Your word is a lamp for my feet, a light on my path.
PSALM 119:105 NIV

• •

Life is busy, isn't it? Most of us have jobs, careers, and obligations that take us away from home for a big chunk of the week, then we have to balance the rest of our time with family, friends, and church and hopefully have a little time to relax. (If your kids are young, this all becomes much more challenging.) In our normal squeeze for time, one of the first casualties is time alone with God in prayer and Bible reading.

The psalmist who wrote today's scripture verse understood that the Word of God gives believers direction and lights the way as we follow its leading. But the apostle Paul had much more to say about what the Bible does for us: "All Scripture is God-breathed and is useful for teaching, rebuking, correcting and training in righteousness, so that the servant of God may be thoroughly equipped for every good work" (2 Timothy 3:16–17 NIV).

So the words recorded in scripture lead and guide us, teach us, rebuke and correct us, and show us what it means to be righteous. Can there be any question as to how important it is that we spend time reading God's Word?

Reading books and other material about the Bible is a good thing, and attending group Bible studies is of tremendous value. But nothing should ever take the place of spending time alone with God, reading and meditating on His written Word.

Father, how easy it is to sacrifice our time on the altar of busyness! We need time alone with You undistracted, and You Yourself want to spend that time with us. Help us to remember the honor that is!

Your Conscience Can Be Your Guide

Holding on to faith and a good conscience, which some have
rejected and so have suffered shipwreck with regard to the faith.
1 TIMOTHY 1:19 NIV

• •

God has given human beings the wonderful gift of a conscience—a sense of right and wrong. But the human conscience was exposed to damage when sin entered into the human experience, when Adam and Eve chose to disobey the one commandment God had given them (Genesis 3). Since that moment, sin has damaged the conscience of every human being. You see it in the early years of a child's life when they know they've done something they had to hide!

When you first received the free gift of salvation through Jesus Christ, God placed His Holy Spirit within you. Part of the Holy Spirit's role in your Christian life is to alert you when you're about to make a choice that doesn't please God. That's partly what Jesus meant when He told His followers that the Spirit would "guide you into all the truth" (John 16:13 NIV). The Holy Spirit refreshes and enlivens our corrupted conscience.

When God's Holy Spirit is inside you, He allows you to better understand the truths of scripture, which are the basis for every decision we make. And when we have the Spirit playing that role in our lives, we can safely allow our conscience to be our guide.

God my Father, thank You for the gift of a conscience and even more
for the gift of Your Holy Spirit in my life. Help me to lean on Your Word,
Your Spirit, and Your guidance—and to never offend my own
conscience by trying to evade its conviction.

Learning Contentment

I know what it is to be in need, and I know what it is to have plenty.
I have learned the secret of being content in any and every situation,
whether well fed or hungry, whether living in plenty or in want.
PHILIPPIANS 4:12 NIV

• •

Modern advertisers and marketers have tapped into something about our fallen human nature that makes too many of us easy marks as customers who buy what we don't need and oftentimes can't afford. Much of the time they aim at our kids with messages about self-worth and identity tied to brands and material possessions.

The world around us does all it can to make us believe that we don't have everything we need, and if we're not careful, we can find ourselves falling into attitudes of discontent because we don't have the newest and best things. It takes a lot of effort to counteract the constant barrage.

The apostle Paul had learned that contentment has less to do with his setting in life (he was in a Roman prison when he wrote to the Philippian church), with his possessions (he had few), or with physical provision (he had apparently experienced real hunger) and everything to do with the fact that he was doing what God had called him to do.

Paul is an amazing example of what true contentment looks like. While we too often feel the pangs of discontent because we don't have the latest and best (fill in the blank), Paul knew how to feel content when he didn't even have a place to stay, enough to eat, or safe travels. We need to seek God's help to learn this lesson and pass it along to the next generation.

Father of all good things, only You can give us the ability to enjoy material things in the right context. Help us to hold all things loosely, so that we are content when You take them back. Help us to learn the secret of true contentment and to model it to our kids.

The Importance of Planning

The plans of the diligent lead to profit
as surely as haste leads to poverty.
PROVERBS 21:5 NIV

• •

The concept of *planning* sometimes gets a strong reaction from Christians. Some believers don't think it's important to make a plan because it limits the "freedom" of the Holy Spirit.

Others believe that when God gives a vision for something, they have to plan everything out to the smallest detail so that they don't head out in the wrong direction.

Is either approach necessarily wrong? Like many things in the Word of God, there is usually a point of balance between the readiness to serve when God calls you to move and making sure you have a plan of action under His authority.

There may be times when God directs you to move out immediately as He did with Joseph when the angel instructed him to flee to Egypt to protect the baby Jesus, but in most instances, He expects you to use wisdom to avoid rushing into things. He encourages you to think through a plan and weigh your options. This is profoundly true in raising children. The vast majority of time you spend on your kids will be the result of planning ahead. That plan doesn't make the Spirit's participation obsolete, of course. Prayerfully and humbly submit your planning process to God so that He can guide you in every step you take. You will benefit, as will your family.

God of my future, I know You have plans for me and for my family. You have placed me here as a father and a teacher, as a guide and provider. Give me wisdom and diligence in planning for the success of my children in knowing You.

God Honors Hard Work

*A sluggard's appetite is never filled, but the
desires of the diligent are fully satisfied.*
PROVERBS 13:4 NIV

• •

It might be hard at times to believe it (especially when it's time to get up each Monday morning), but from the very beginning, God intended for man to work. His first assignment for Adam was to live in the Garden of Eden and "to work it and take care of it" (Genesis 2:15 NIV). Sadly, when Adam and Eve sinned, work turned into toil—and it has been that way ever since (Genesis 3).

But the fact still remains that it's God's will that each man work and produce. Not only that, He warns against laziness and encourages us to work hard, with diligence as working unto the Lord. Proverbs tells us that laziness leads to poverty and that those who demonstrate diligence in their work will find that their needs are met.

And as you work, remember that you are providing more than food and shelter for your family, but an example of serving the Lord as well. "Whatever you do, work heartily, as for the Lord and not for men, knowing that from the Lord you will receive the inheritance as your reward. You are serving the Lord Christ" (Colossians 3:23–24 ESV).

*O Lord, my Provider, You designed me to work and allowed
me to serve You in any job I take. I praise You that my work
matters and is an opportunity to worship You all week long!*

Living with Integrity

*At this, the administrators and the satraps tried to find grounds
for charges against Daniel in his conduct of government affairs,
but they were unable to do so. They could find no corruption in him,
because he was trustworthy and neither corrupt nor negligent.*
DANIEL 6:4 NIV

. . . .

The famous Christian motivational speaker Zig Ziglar once said, "With integrity, you have nothing to fear, since you have nothing to hide. With integrity, you will do the right thing, so you will have no guilt."

The Old Testament prophet Daniel—who was only a teenager when he was taken as a captive to Babylon—demonstrated integrity in every part of his life. He honored God—and God honored the prophet in return . . .and also saved him from becoming some hungry lion's lunch (Daniel 6:10–23).

Daniel had his enemies, but it turns out he had nothing to fear, simply because he had conducted all his affairs in a way that honored and pleased his God.

You honor and please God and establish a good reputation with others when you make sure you live every part of your life with integrity. And as you do, your children will see it. Remember, it's never too early or too late to live in integrity.

*God of truth, You enjoy seeing me live in integrity because it means
I'm living like Christ: unafraid of the consequences in this world.
Give me courage to live my life for Your approval only and to
deal honestly and consistently as an ambassador for Christ.*

Being "Real" with God

Immediately the boy's father exclaimed,
"I do believe; help me overcome my unbelief!"
MARK 9:24 NIV

• •

It's amazing how desperation can often bring out the best in people. When the chips are down and when our backs are against the wall (pick your own cliché here), we're often forced to get real with one another. . . and with God.

The father in Mark 9:24 was at a point where he had no choice but to turn to Jesus for help. He apparently knew enough about Jesus to know that He had miraculously healed many people. But it is equally apparent that he had his doubts as to whether Jesus could help *him*.

Jesus responded to this father's kernel of faith. . .and to his honesty. He healed the man's son and then used the incident to teach His followers some things about real, mountain-moving, demon-repelling faith.

Jesus repeatedly and consistently taught His followers that they could do anything if they had faith. Those same promises hold true for us today. But in those times when we wonder if we have "enough" faith, when we wonder if God can reach down and make a difference in our lives, our best first step might be to confess honestly, "I do believe, Lord. Help me overcome my unbelief."

O God, how I feel for the father in this passage! There is nothing I would not do to see my children whole, but I need Your strength to really understand faith. Thank You that You do not disdain me when I cry out for help just to believe.

Forgive Yourself!

• •

As fathers, there's always something we would do differently if we had the chance to go back in time. That's normal because we are all growing and learning, and we all make mistakes. But for some of us, it's hard to let go of the guilt associated with our past. We walk around filled with regret, believing deep down that even though we've given ourselves over to Jesus Christ, God still intends to lower the boom on us for our past sins.

The Bible calls our spiritual enemy, Satan, the "accuser of our brothers and sisters" (Revelation 12:10 NIV) and a "liar" (John 8:44), and he loves few things more than tormenting believers with reminders of their sinful pasts. If the Holy Spirit is convicting you to apologize or make amends, that's different. That's part of walking with Christ today, not living under the burden of the past. The Bible tells us that there is no condemnation for those of us who belong to Jesus and that our sins are forgiven and buried in a sea of divine forgetfulness (Micah 7:19). This is where God intends for us to live—free from guilt and free to do what's right.

So no matter what you've done in your past, no matter how awful a sinner you believe you were before Jesus found you, forgave you, and cleansed you, forgive yourself. Let go of your sinful past (God already has) and move on into the wonderful, full life God has given you through the sacrifice of His Son.

*Father of our souls, You alone can bring us to freedom—
both from sin and from the guilt of sin. We need both, O Lord!
Help us to believe in Your promises of forgiveness and life.
And help us to extend the grace we receive to others.*

Being Patient with God

Wait for the LORD; be strong and take heart and wait for the LORD.
PSALM 27:14 NIV

• •

It's so commonly spoken that it's become something of a Christian cliché, but in light of today's scripture verse, it bears repeating here: "God answers prayers in one of three ways—yes, no, and not yet." It really shouldn't surprise us though—isn't that the way we, as earthly fathers, answer our children?

Of course, our kids *always* want a yes, and we're no different, though as adults we can even understand why He says no. sometimes. But that "not yet"—that one can really mess with us. When we pray for something we know is God's will (say, the salvation of a loved one or personal spiritual revival), we're often flummoxed when it doesn't happen right away. So we keep praying—sometimes over a period of years—and waiting.

The scriptural truth of the matter is that God often makes His people wait before He answers their requests. We may not understand why we have to wait, so we must cling to the truth that God's ways and thoughts are different from ours (Isaiah 55:8).

So be patient and keep seeking God. He has made literally hundreds of promises in scripture, and His track record of keeping them still stands at 100 percent.

Our part of this grand bargain is to wait patiently, knowing that God's very nature keeps Him from letting us down. He's a good and wise Father.

Gentle Father, You do want us to ask You for all the things in our hearts. But You are too wise and too caring to simply grant everything in the way and the time we want. Help us to trust in You as we wait upon Your timing and far better judgment.

Enjoying Inner Peace

Great peace have those who love your law,
and nothing can make them stumble.
PSALM 119:165 NIV

• •

One of the great promises of the Gospel message is peace. Somehow, though, many have interpreted that promise as meaning that a believer's life will be free of troubles and concerns, that God will somehow rid us of all our problems when we commit ourselves to Him.

But nowhere in the Bible will you receive any promise of peace in terms of what life throws your way. The Bible warns that we all have to endure our share of storms and crises. Failing health, rebellious children, rocky marriages, job layoffs—the list is endless. Jesus wasn't kidding when He said, "In this world you will have trouble" (John 16:33 NIV).

But this same Jesus said, "Peace I leave with you; my peace I give you. I do not give to you as the world gives. Do not let your hearts be troubled and do not be afraid" (John 14:27 NIV).

Jesus wanted His followers to understand that peace isn't about a lack of problems in this world, but about the inner tranquility His followers can and should enjoy even in the most difficult of times.

We enjoy God's inner peace when we do two things: commit to walking with Him daily as His true disciples, and focus on Him and not our outer circumstances when we are going through difficult times.

Father, I need Your strength to face what comes in this life—I need
Your peace! I know You love me and are with me, but sometimes I can't
always remember that when trouble comes. Help me to lean on You with
the faith Jesus did when He faced all this world could throw at Him.

Strength through Tribulations

Not only so, but we also glory in our sufferings,
because we know that suffering produces perseverance.
ROMANS 5:3 NIV

• •

If we had to guess what words flowed through the pen of the apostle Paul following today's verse, we might try this: "What doesn't kill you makes you stronger."

Of course that's not what Paul wrote, but it might make for a good summary for what he actually jotted down. He actually wrote that perseverance produces "character; and character, hope. And hope does not put us to shame, because God's love has been poured out into our hearts through the Holy Spirit, who has been given to us" (Romans 5:4–5 NIV).

Right! We might think after reading those words, *What doesn't kill me truly can make me stronger.*

Paul knew as well as anyone that God could and did use his suffering and tribulation (and he endured more than his share of both during his ministry) to strengthen him and to give him the character and drive it took to endure whatever a hostile world threw at him. This can be a tough lesson to learn, and a tougher one to pass on to our kids. But it's important to spiritual growth—in adult and child alike—to understand suffering and endurance from a spiritual perspective. Just as an athlete's training regimen tears his body down but later makes it stronger and more fit for competition, tribulation can make us stronger, more Christlike, and better fit for the work God has given us to do. Let's embrace those trainable moments in ourselves and our children so we grow from them and don't miss the opportunity to turn something painful into something useful.

Father, You train me for my own good and for Your glory.
Help me to seek You in that moment when I am
tempted to run away, and trust You for the outcome.

Gossip—Stop It!

A gossip betrays a confidence,
but a trustworthy person keeps a secret.
PROVERBS 11:13 NIV

• •

Gossip is one of those all-too-common sins that we might think of as a "little one"—certainly not on par with the "biggies" like adultery, murder, or theft. But long before a person is tempted to the "biggies," he's practiced the "little ones!" And gossip comes as easy as breathing. Kids do it naturally; adults do it intentionally. But what's the "big" deal about this "little" sin?

When you look at what the Bible has to say about gossip, you'll find that God takes it very, very seriously. In the first chapter of Paul's letter to the Romans, he writes about God's punishment on sinful humans for their lawlessness. He goes on to provide a list of sinful individuals whose behavior makes them deserving of God's judgment. Right there in verse 29 is the word *gossips*.

Let's get real with ourselves here. God hates gossip, and He hates it because it destroys what He has created and has worked so hard to restore and protect—the name of another person.

So let's be very careful not just what we say *to* another person, but also what we say *about* him or her. Let's think before we speak about another. Let's ask ourselves first if what we are about to say is true. Then let's ask ourselves if our words are loving and helpful. . .or if they just damage another's reputation.

And if the words we are about to speak don't pass muster, let's keep them to ourselves.

Father of encouragement, catch me in my habit of gossip!
It's so easy to speak negatively of others when I'm focused
on myself. Help me to honor You in every conversation and
to encourage others rather than destroy them.

Seeing God in Creation

*"But ask the animals, and they will teach you, or the birds in the sky,
and they will tell you; or speak to the earth, and it will teach you,
or let the fish in the sea inform you. Which of all these does
not know that the hand of the LORD has done this?"*
JOB 12:7–9 NIV

• •

There are all kinds of settings in which you can spend time with God and enjoy His presence. Today's verse teaches us that we can see the greatness of God and experience His presence in a setting too few of us get to enjoy these days: in nature.

The natural world is a perfect environment to introduce your children to God, the Creator of all things. Ask believers who enjoy spending time outdoors (hiking, camping, fishing, hunting, and other activities), and they'll likely tell you that natural settings are places where they see God's greatness and creativity, where they communicate with Him. . .and where He communicates with them.

Job certainly understood this truth. He had apparently pondered the greatness of God in the natural world around him.

Your time with God in a natural setting should never take the place of time spent in fellowship with other believers, and it should never crowd out "quiet time" spent reading God's Word and praying. But, as Job points out, you can find great blessing in seeing God's handiwork and experience His presence when you spend time enjoying creation and everything in it.

*Father, You display Your power and Your wisdom through all of
Your vast creation. You provided for everyone at all times
a glimpse of Your glory through nature. Thank You for Your
attention to detail and for making all things beautiful.*

Feeling Small?

*When I consider your heavens, the work of your fingers, the moon
and the stars, which you have set in place, what is mankind that
you are mindful of them, human beings that you care for them?*
PSALM 8:3–4 NIV

• •

The naturalist William Beebe and his good friend President Theodore
Roosevelt went for a walk together one night after dinner. Roosevelt
pointed skyward and observed, "That is the Spiral Galaxy in Andromeda.
It is as large as our Milky Way. It is one of a hundred billion galaxies. It
consists of one hundred billion stars, each larger than our sun. Now I
think we are small enough. Let's go to bed."

King David lived thousands of years before modern telescopes, so
he had no real clue as to the vastness of the created universe. Still, what
he *could* observe with his naked eye still astonished him. But even more
amazing to him was the fact that the God who had created it all could
look down from His throne in heaven and not just take notice of him, but
love him and desire a relationship with him. King David, from his youth
as a shepherd, understood the vast love of God the Father from the vast
scale of creation.

That's a wonderful thought, isn't it? That the all-powerful God who
created such a vast cosmos is the same all-loving Father who cares so
deeply for each of us. To God, the cosmos is small and we His children
are large!

*Father Creator, the universe displays Your endless power as a gift to
mankind. As earthly fathers work to provide a place that may never
be fully appreciated by their children, so You have provided an entire
cosmos that we might comprehend Your great love a little better.*

Kingdom Work—Just Keep at It!

*Let us not become weary in doing good, for at the
proper time we will reap a harvest if we do not give up.*
GALATIANS 6:9 NIV

• •

Think of some of the great preachers in Christian history. From the apostles
Peter and Paul all the way through the centuries to men like Billy Graham,
certain preachers are exceptional in our eyes because the results of their
work are both obvious and tremendous.

But it's not like that for every kingdom laborer. For some of us it's more
like teaching a kid to clean his room—lots of effort with no discernible
results!

God never promised us that working for Him would be easy—or
that we'd see a huge harvest of souls or large numbers of lives changed
through that work. We don't always see the results of our hard work
for the kingdom of God in the short run; in fact, we may not see them
at all this side of heaven. But Galatians 6:9 promises us that if we
persevere in our good work for the Lord, we *will* share with Him in the
joy of seeing the furthering of His eternal kingdom.

So when you begin to wonder whether you're making a difference in
the world around you, don't give up. Just keep doing what God has laid
on your heart to do, and He'll take care of the rest.

*God of the Harvest, we know You have a plan for us and a place
to work in Your harvest. We long to see the results of our work,
but we also trust You to accomplish Your results in Your time.
Keep us faithful, Father, to serve diligently and patiently.*

The Father's Delight

*"The LORD your God is with you, the Mighty Warrior who saves.
He will take great delight in you; in his love he will no longer
rebuke you, but will rejoice over you with singing."*
ZEPHANIAH 3:17 NIV

• •

The Old Testament prophet Zephaniah wrote his prophecy during a very difficult time for the nation of Israel. His message is one of coming judgments on God's chosen people. But the book ends with wonderful promises of restoration—restoration of the loving, close relationship between God and His people. The restoration of the Father to His children.

The third chapter of Zephaniah is a series of promises and encouragements, all of which God directs at His people today. It tells us that God isn't just a God who loves His people but also a God who takes delight in us—such delight that His heart breaks out in song.

The promises in today's scripture verse point to a time when God " 'will wipe every tear from their eyes. There will be no more death' or mourning or crying or pain, for the old order of things has passed away" (Revelation 21:4 NIV).

This is the beginning of eternal life in the paradise that is heaven, the beginning of an eternity in the presence of the One who will no longer correct or rebuke us—and who will celebrate our presence as much as we do His.

*Father, You delight over us! It's hard to imagine until
we remember how we feel over our own children when
there are no barriers between us. Thank You, Father,
for Your patience and love that leads to our restoration.*

A Most Important Command

Whoever claims to love God yet hates a brother or sister is a liar.
For whoever does not love their brother and sister, whom they have seen,
cannot love God, whom they have not seen. And he has given us this
command: Anyone who loves God must also love their brother and sister.
1 JOHN 4:20–21 NIV

• •

Let's face it: Some people are very difficult to love. They're too loud, too opinionated, too overbearing, too unlearned, too selfish, etc. You could try to avoid them, but sometimes they're in your own family! But the apostle John has some very strong words as to how we as followers of Christ are to relate to even the most unlovable among us.

If you can't love someone who's right in front of you, John taught, *then how can you say you love a God you can't even see?* That's putting John's message rhetorically, for of course the answer is that saying we love God but not the people He's placed in our lives makes us. . .well, liars.

Ouch!

So when you encounter the "unlovable"—and there are plenty of them out there!—love them the way Jesus loved, unconditionally and sacrificially. And when your words and acts of love don't change them in the least, love them all the more. It's God's job to change people—it's your job to love them the same way He loves you.

Father, I need Your perspective on the unlovable people around me.
Maybe I'm one of those people to someone else! Teach me to act
according to love, not according to my own feelings. And show
me where I may be making it difficult for others to love me.

Divine Forgetfulness

"I, even I, am he who blots out your transgressions,
for my own sake, and remembers your sins no more."
ISAIAH 43:25 NIV

• •

If you think about it, part of the message behind today's verse might seem to contradict the very nature of God. Sure, we can grasp—and celebrate in—the fact that God forgives our sins and cleanses us from all unrighteousness. But how can a God who knows everything that has happened or will happen in eternity past and in eternity future forget something?

Let's put this in human perspective for just a moment. Suppose your spouse or child or someone else close to you does or says something to cause you pain or loss. It may be a matter of simple carelessness, or it could have been something done intentionally. Either way, you've decided that it is far better to forgive that person and restore the relationship than it is to cling to wrongs done and let it die. You can't literally forget the offense committed, but you can forget any thought of punishing that person for what he or she has done to you.

God's "forgetfulness" is a lot like that. He remembers sins we've committed against Him, but when we come to Him in humble repentance, He forgives us and casts away any thought of vengeance against us.

What joy to have a forgetful Father! You have made a way that
allows us to have a relationship with You—by forgetting our sins.
We rejoice in Your love and that You want us as Your children.
Thank You for forgetting the hurt we've caused You!

Choosing Friends Wisely

Do not make friends with a hot-tempered person,
do not associate with one easily angered, or you
may learn their ways and get yourself ensnared.
PROVERBS 22:24–25 NIV

• •

People with bad tempers can be very unpleasant to be around. Sure, they can be good company—as long as other people and life itself are treating them the way they deserve to be treated. But when some offense comes, the ill-tempered can react with unkind words and unkind (or even violent or dangerous) actions.

The Bible includes some simple but very sound wisdom when it comes to dealing with hot-tempered people: stay clear! Sure, we're going to encounter people with bad tempers (and other sinful attitudes and behaviors), but today's passage advises us to avoid socializing too much with these kinds of people.

Our God is all-knowing and all-wise, and He understands far better than we do that we tend to adopt the behaviors of those closest to us. He also knows that a person with a bad temper is headed for disaster, and He will do everything He can to make sure His children don't end up in the same place. And why not? We do the same thing with our kids. Every parent wants to know what kind of friends their children are hanging out with and whether that will be healthy for them in the long run. (And to be fair, we need to watch out that it's not our kid the other parents don't want around!)

It's a simple bit of wisdom: don't spend your time with a hothead!

Father of peace, You have us, and our children, in a world that is
corrupt and sometimes dangerous. Help us to be wise about
the company we keep so that we are not influenced by them
but instead become an influence to bring them into Your kingdom.

One-on-One Interventions

*Better is open rebuke than hidden love. Wounds from
a friend can be trusted, but an enemy multiplies kisses.*
PROVERBS 27:5–6 NIV

• •

Raising kids is built on correction and training, discipline and teaching,
sometimes rebuke. It's perfectly natural and ultimately healthy. But as
adults it gets more complicated. Confrontation is uncomfortable for most
people. We don't like being told that we're harboring sinful or unhealthy
attitudes or taking part in actions that displease God or cause others
pain. And it can be even harder to be "that guy"—the one who must
somehow summon the courage it takes to confront a friend who so
desperately needs it.

But the Bible tells us that a true friend is one who is willing to risk
the friendship and say what needs to be said to a brother or sister in the
Lord who is either living with obvious sin or has some kind of blind spot
that keeps him or her from living or thinking in a way that pleases God.

It's easy to decide to just mind your own business when your friend
strays from God's standards of living and thinking. But today's verse
teaches us that part of being a real friend is being willing, no matter how
uncomfortable it may be, to speak difficult truth to those you love—and
to do it gently and firmly.

Do you have that kind of friend? And can you be that kind of friend?

*Father, I need rebuke, but it's so hard to take! My pride gets in the
way—I don't like being vulnerable and I don't like seeming weak.
Help me to be humble to receive correction since it all comes from You.
And teach me to speak with gentleness to those I correct.*

"I'll Pray for You"

"My intercessor is my friend as my eyes pour out tears to God;
on behalf of a man he pleads with God as one pleads for a friend."
JOB 16:20-21 NIV

• •

The Bible has a lot to teach us about how to pray, when to pray, and what to pray for. One type of prayer the Word tells us to engage in regularly is called *intercession*, which is a type of prayer in which we "stand in the gap" before God on behalf of another person.

But just how important is it to God that His people intercede in prayer for others? So important that Jesus, His very own Son, spends His time in heaven interceding for us this very moment (Hebrews 7:23–28).

When a spouse or child, friend or coworker, or another brother or sister in Christ is hurting and in need of a touch from the hand of God, it's always good to offer comfort by promising to pray for that person. But as you spend time with the Lord, please be sure to make good on that promise. God loves to answer His people's prayers, and He is absolutely delighted to answer prayers of loving concern when we offer them up to Him.

So don't forget to make intercession for others—especially your family—a regular part of your prayer life. Someone may very well be counting on you.

Lord, You are working on the earth through the prayers of Your people. How great an opportunity for us to be part of Your kingdom! Teach us to be faithful in lifting up others, in interceding the way Christ does for us.

Friends with God

"I no longer call you servants, because a servant does not know his master's business. Instead, I have called you friends, for everything that I learned from my Father I have made known to you."
JOHN 15:15 NIV

• •

We all want our kids to develop healthy friendships. We want the right influences since " 'Bad company corrupts good character' " (1 Corinthians 15:33 NIV). And we want our children to be good friends to others, learning how to share, listen, and serve.

There's something special about the work we do in helping our friends. There's something about getting our hands dirty in simple tasks like helping someone move or spending a Saturday helping him with some chore, or in more "emotional" ways like offering a listening ear during times of trouble, that brings you closer to your friend. We grow when we serve, and our kids learn when they see it in action.

The same is true of the greatest Friend any of us will ever know—Jesus, who demonstrated His love for His friends by laying down His own life for us (John 15:13). When we walk closely with Him, listen to Him, and follow His leading, He calls us His own friends (John 15:14).

Jesus is such a loving Friend that He walked the earth for more than thirty years for us, taught us, died for us, was raised from the grave for us, and now resides in heaven, where He constantly pleads our case before His heavenly Father (Hebrews 7:25).

As the old hymn says, "What a Friend we have in Jesus!" Let's show our kids this most unique of friends!

Father, You invented friendship and demonstrated it to the uttermost. We can only marvel at being called Your Son's friends! Help us to be good friends to Him and to cherish that friendship in all that we say and do.

This Is Life

*"Now this is eternal life: that they know you,
the only true God, and Jesus Christ, whom you have sent."*
JOHN 17:3 NIV

. . . .

We've all seen those T-shirts bearing the none-too-profound message that "Football is Life," "Baseball is Life," or "Basketball is Life."

There are a lot of easily observable things about American culture, and one of them is that we are absolutely obsessed with sports—youth and high school sports (especially for those of us who have children competing), college sports, and professional sports alike.

There's nothing wrong with enjoying spectator sports—as long as you put them in their proper place in your life. These things are not life, just an enjoyable part of it. When they become an obsession, when they dominate your thinking and the way you live, then they become idols—and we know how God feels about idols!

For the believer, life isn't the work we do, the recreation we enjoy on the weekends, or the sports teams we follow. Real life—abundant life and everlasting life—is found in knowing God through Jesus Christ, the One He sent so that we could live eternally.

So feel free to root for your team and to enjoy watching a game. But never forget that these things don't define or make your life.

God, thank You for creating things for us to enjoy and that make our lives full, especially as families. But help us to remember that above all, knowing You through Your Son is the way to experience real life.

Your Place in the Big Picture

What, after all, is Apollos? And what is Paul? Only servants, through whom you came to believe—as the Lord has assigned to each his task. I planted the seed, Apollos watered it, but God has been making it grow.
1 CORINTHIANS 3:5–6 NIV

• •

Read most every list of the most important/influential people in the history of Western civilization, and you're likely to find the name of the apostle Paul mentioned prominently. Of course, Paul was largely responsible for spreading Christianity throughout the known world, and we can't forget that he wrote most of the New Testament.

The people Paul reached personally saw him as an apostle and a spiritual father, and his "children" in the faith held him in the highest esteem. Paul poured himself out for the Church and ultimately gave his life for the work of Christ.

But you only need to read today's scripture passage to know that Paul's response to being held in such high esteem in such a list would be along the lines of, "I'm nobody!" Paul understood that God had given him a big assignment, but he also understood that it was God, not him, who was worthy of the glory for the results.

God has given us, His servants, responsibilities that are but small parts in the bigger plan of salvation for others. Our job is to sow the seeds by telling others the truth about salvation through Jesus Christ and to water those seeds through prayer. God's part is to illuminate the message we present (to make the seed grow) and bring people to Him through the work of His Holy Spirit.

Father, we thank You for the blessing of serving our families, our church, and our world, but growth comes only from You! We want only to be faithful servants. We rejoice in Your salvation, Your kingdom, and Your working through us in the world!

Character First

"Blessed are you when people insult you, persecute you
and falsely say all kinds of evil against you because of me."
MATTHEW 5:11 NIV

• •

The great basketball coach John Wooden once said, "Be more concerned with your character than your reputation, because your character is what you really are, while your reputation is merely what others think you are."

Wooden's words point out the simple truth that character and reputation, while they are closely related, are not the same thing. Ideally, a life defined by godly character—the kind of life committed to treating people well, conducting business with integrity, building a family with true love, and worshipping God in both word and deed—will lead to a good reputation. Or as Proverbs 22:1 (NIV) calls it, "a good name." But there's no guarantee.

There are few things in life that are worth guarding with great passion, and one of those is character. From that, you can establish a good reputation by making sure that the thoughts you think, the words you speak, and the actions you take are those that please God in every way. But character always comes first.

Father, You are committed to my character and not worried so much
about my reputation. Help me to keep in step with Your Spirit
and to do all I can to maintain a "good name," but no matter what
others may say about me, help me to only listen to Your opinion.

Stop Your Griping!

Do everything without grumbling or arguing, so that you may become blameless and pure, "children of God without fault in a warped and crooked generation."
PHILIPPIANS 2:14–15 NIV

. . . .

If you think about it, from the moment we are born and the doctor slaps us on the bottom, we start complaining. *Hey! That's not fair!* And it doesn't get any easier.

You don't have to teach your kids to grumble—it's preprogrammed. Going to school, doing chores, finishing homework. . .and don't even try to get them on a bedtime schedule! With time, we hope to train our kids not to complain, but taking an honest look at ourselves, can we say we've really outgrown it?

While the Bible contains some examples of godly men who complained to God (David and Job, for example), it also warns us against grumbling and complaining, and it shows us that having a complaining attitude and mouth can have very negative consequences (Numbers 14).

When we complain, we separate ourselves from God and His peace, and we also ruin our testimony for Christ to a lost and hurting world. After all, who wants to listen to someone offering answers when that person constantly gripes about his own life?

So in those times when you don't think life is being fair to you, remember to do as the apostle Paul instructed and "give thanks in all circumstances; for this is God's will for you in Christ Jesus" (1 Thessalonians 5:18 NIV). Also remember God's promise that "in all things God works for the good of those who love him, who have been called according to his purpose" (Romans 8:28 NIV).

Heavenly Father, help us to see beyond the temporary and to return thanks as children who appreciate You and all You've done.

Giving—with the Right Motives

*"So when you give to the needy, do not announce it with trumpets,
as the hypocrites do in the synagogues and on the streets, to be
honored by others. Truly I tell you, they have received their reward in full."*
MATTHEW 6:2 NIV

• •

Everyone likes to be recognized for their efforts. Little league trophies, 5K T-shirts, office plaques, newspaper articles—you name it. But there are some arenas that recognition can be a spiritual problem. We may not want to admit it, but it can be easy to wonder, *What's in it for me?* when we think of giving to others. Jesus understood this part of fallen human nature, and that's why He told His followers not to seek human recognition when we give.

When we think of the word *giving*, our minds usually go to the financial. But God also calls us to give of our time, of our efforts, of any other of the gifts He's given us. But no matter what we find ourselves in a position to give, the principle stands the same. When we give, we're to do it in a way so that only God—and sometimes the recipient—knows about it.

So give—give generously. But when you give, make sure your heart and mind are free of any desire for human recognition or any other earthly reward. When you give with a pure heart that is motivated by the desire to glorify God and bless others, God will honor your giving and bless you in return.

*Father, You are the Giver of all things, the only One
who deserves recognition and praise. Help us to give
generously and secretly so that we participate in Your
work, without getting in the way of Your glory.*

Thank God It's Monday!

This is the day which the LORD has made;
let us rejoice and be glad in it.
PSALM 118:24 NASB

• •

Some men only tolerate their jobs because it pays the bills and it's better than being unemployed. It could be called a kind of perseverance, but it's really more of a survival approach to work. Other men like their work, though sometimes when the workload is heavy, the pressure intense, or coworkers unpleasant, even normally enjoyable employment becomes drudgery. It's no surprise many guys don't look forward to Monday morning. The weekend that promised relief is fading away and irritability rises; perhaps short-tempered responses to the kids follow or impatience with a spouse. All signs we've misplaced our hope. That's why men need to pause in the morning to commit the day to God in prayer.

Jesus said, "Don't worry about tomorrow, for tomorrow will bring its own worries. Today's trouble is enough for today" (Matthew 6:34 NLT). But the point is: Christians shouldn't even fret about today. There *is* trouble enough for today, but God's power is enough to handle every bit of that trouble. God has made this day, and He supplies the grace to face it. Men don't need to just grit their teeth and bear it. They can be glad in it. One time, Nehemiah's workers were discouraged by steady conflict and worn out by the immensity of their tasks, so Nehemiah encouraged them, saying, "The joy of the LORD is your strength" (Nehemiah 8:10 NKJV). They couldn't rejoice in their troubles, but they *could* rejoice in the Lord. Like them, if we continually remind ourselves that the all-powerful God is with us, we can literally rejoice—even if it's Monday.

Father, You are the Father of Monday as well as the weekend!
Help me to pause every day to remember Your great love and promises!

Solid and Steady

Tell the older men to have self-control and to be serious and sensible.
Their faith, love, and patience must never fail.
TITUS 2:2 CEV

• •

As they get older, most men naturally become more serious and sensible. In fact, a common complaint is that old men are overly serious and practical. They've lost their sense of fun and adventure to such an extent that they become *unreasonably* sensible, if such a thing can be. At least, that's what many younger men think. But while older Christian men should retain a zest for life and be able to lighten up at times, God intended them to be steady pillars of their families, societies, and churches. Some things—such as serving God—are *meant* to be taken seriously.

Advancing age tends to bring about this change in men, but full maturity still requires effort on their part. They must also have exercised a lifetime of self-control. For many people, sexual purity comes to mind when they think of self-control, and this is an important aspect of it, but self-control must extend to every area of a man's life. He must also govern any tendency toward greed or selfishness; he must constantly exercise control over his temper; he must maintain a daily habit of prayer and devotions. Victory in all these areas doesn't happen overnight. It takes years of faithfulness and self-discipline, but it's worth it in the long haul. If a man does these things and *continues* doing them as he gets older, his patience, his love, and his faith will never fail. He and his family, his church and his friends will all be the richer for his efforts.

Father, You are the source of our strength and our faithfulness.
Only in You can we be consistent, sensible, and a blessing to others.
As we get older, Father, show us how to pass along what we've
learned, so we can leave a legacy to the next generation.

Knowing What You Believe

*Always be prepared to give an answer to everyone who
asks you to give the reason for the hope that you have.
But do this with gentleness and respect.*
1 PETER 3:15 NIV

• •

Men who love baseball usually develop an impressive level of expertise on the subject. They're self-taught, yes, but they often know all the players on their favorite teams, how many home runs each one has made, their batting averages, etc. And it doesn't take much prompting to get them to talk enthusiastically about the subject. The same applies to men who are passionate about politics: they have strong, well-informed, clearly defined opinions, and they don't hesitate to share them with people of opposing viewpoints.

The Bible tells believers that they should be the same way about their faith—though not necessarily to the degree of detail a teenager might discuss music. But with gentleness and respect, believers should always be prepared to give an answer and explain why they believe. Many men, however, know surprisingly little about their faith, though the remedy is pretty straightforward. They must study their Bibles. This may seem like a daunting task, but it will be easy if they're as passionate about God as they are about baseball or politics. Once they're fascinated by the message of Jesus, they gladly immerse themselves in it. It's not a chore. It's a joy. And as they read and spend time praying over it, they discover countless truths. Then, explaining what they believe comes easy. Even if they're "only" self-taught, if they're full of their subject, they'll be prepared to give a reason.

*Heavenly Father, prepare our hearts to receive Your
message as we read our Bibles daily. Help us to
develop the habit of listening to You in Your Word.*

Shifting Out of Work Mode

Better to be patient than powerful; better to
have self-control than to conquer a city.
PROVERBS 16:32 NLT

• •

Men are generally purpose-driven, goal-oriented beings. God designed us this way so that we concentrate on our life's mission. We're literally hardwired to be focused and ambitious, and these traits impel us toward success. But some of us focus inordinately on building a career—like a heat-seeking missile locked on target, we ignore all distractions. This can be a good thing—except when those "distractions" are our wives and children. That's why a man must learn to consciously shift gears when the day ends and leave his work at work. A proper context for "work mode" is necessary so we don't walk through the door at home still trying to solve work problems and tune out our family. If we can't balance the workplace drive, we can become impatient when our wives require our attention or our children make demands on our time.

Now, our business may be focused on conquering the city, and our job may make serious demands of us, but on the drive home we should exercise self-control and refocus on those dearest to us. We must truly value and be thankful for the wife God has given each of us. We must realize that success is not only defined by a job well done, but by our love and care for our children. It often takes effort to focus on the home scene. It takes self-control to keep our thoughts from drifting back to a work problem. But the rewards and joys that come from giving undivided attention to our families make the effort well worth it.

Father, how good it is to know You never push us aside for "work"
issues! You are always patient and interested. Help us, as fathers
and husbands, to balance our work and our families properly.
Keep reminding us of the things that are most valuable for eternity.

Wait for the Lord

Wait for the LORD; be strong and let your
heart take courage; yes, wait for the LORD.
PSALM 27:14 NASB

• •

It can be maddening when a situation demands immediate action, yet you're not able to do a thing. Things are out of control, and you have the sickening feeling that they're *not* going to end well. The roof might be caving in on an important project at work, or a family situation is going from bad to worse. The kids may be causing stress in your marriage because they know how to pit you and your wife against each other. The pressure on you as a leader builds, demanding that you think of *something*, that you do *something*. But you've already tried everything, and nothing works.

At times like this, the best thing to do is pray. Commit your problem into God's hands then wait for Him to act. That's sometimes a very difficult thing to do, because you've learned by now that God doesn't always have your sense of priorities or work according to your schedule. Yet twice in this one short verse it says, "Wait for the LORD." And while you're waiting, "be strong." Don't give up. Don't throw in the towel, but "let your heart take courage." And the best way to have courage is to trust that God is going to answer prayer and resolve the situation.

Things may continue to look hopeless for a while, but God will come through for you. He will either inspire you with a solution you hadn't thought of before, or He Himself will do a miracle to solve the problem. So take courage. Wait for the Lord.

Gracious God, my Father, my Hope, help me to lean on You rather
than my own understanding! Apart from You I can do nothing
lasting or good; only You can bring about Your kingdom. Help me
to wait upon You to see Your will done rather than mine.

Honest, Sincere Christianity

"The seeds that fell on the good soil represent honest, good-hearted people who hear God's word, cling to it, and patiently produce a huge harvest."
LUKE 8:15 NLT

• •

Many people are so used to thinking that the parable of the sower describes salvation that they miss its other important lessons. Now, it does talk about getting saved, but the moment of salvation is part of a larger picture. Jesus didn't intend for you to simply get a ticket to heaven then shift into cruise mode until you die. It's more like having kids: bringing them into the world is just the start! Being saved is the same: it's the beginning of an entirely new lifestyle, where "honest, good-hearted people" who accept the Gospel then set out to live it. You must not only hear God's Word, but cling tenaciously to it, and as a result produce good fruit that stands the test of time. And it comes from hearing and obeying the words of Jesus. Moses told the children of Israel, "Take to heart all the words I have solemnly declared to you this day. . . . They are not just idle words for you—they are your life" (Deuteronomy 32:46–47 NIV). And this is true for you today as well. You are to be "nourished in the words of faith and of the good doctrine which you have carefully followed" (1 Timothy 4:6 NKJV). You should not only *hear* God's Word, but be spiritually nourished by it, cling to it, and carefully follow its instructions. Have you ever wondered what the secret to a victorious life is? This is it.

Father, You have such a plan for Your children! We get to grow into Your likeness and share in Your holiness! You have blessed us as Your very own, and we want to live as honest, good-hearted people who reflect Your glory.

Natural and Supernatural Talents

[Huram's] father was. . .a skilled craftsman in bronze.
Huram was filled with wisdom, with understanding and
with knowledge to do all kinds of bronze work.
1 KINGS 7:14 NIV

● ●

When the Israelites were in the desert, God chose Bezalel to create all the items for His worship tent. God said, "I have filled him with the Spirit of God, with wisdom, with understanding, with knowledge and with all kinds of skills" (Exodus 31:3 NIV). One of Bezalel's many skills was bronze work. It sounds like God supernaturally anointed Bezalel to do this. But what about Huram? When King Solomon wanted to build God's temple, there was an even greater need for a skilled bronze worker. But God didn't say that Huram's talents were a supernatural gift. In fact, the Bible points out that Huram's *father* was a skilled bronze worker, indicating that Huram had inherited his abilities. They were a natural talent. Plus, his father trained him. That accounted for his knowledge and understanding. But the thing is, even if he was *born* with this talent, it was still a God-given gift. After all, God was the one who wired his DNA and gave him his aptitudes and abilities.

The same applies to you today. You may come from a long line of mechanics and the talent may run in your family, but God is the one who gives such gifts—both to families and to individuals. But it's up to you to work to improve your ability. And when you're praying and seeking to serve God, He gives you an extra anointing to be even more skillful.

Father of all good gifts, thank You for what talents and abilities
You've given to me. I want to honor You with them and grow
them as a good son. Help me to remember that all my skills
and abilities are only from You, and for You.

Serving Others

He sat down, called the twelve disciples over to him,
and said, "Whoever wants to be first must take
last place and be the servant of everyone else."
MARK 9:35 NLT

• •

Many men are leery of the concept of *servanthood*. While they understand the need to love their fellow man and to live honest, virtuous lives, somehow the idea of being a servant of everyone makes no sense. They can understand being helpful, even occasionally going out of their way to lend a hand, but consistently putting others first and themselves last is an alien concept. It doesn't seem practical. Yet Jesus stated this on more than one occasion.

In Mark's Gospel, Jesus said, "Whoever wants to be first must take last place and be the servant of everyone else." This needs to be understood in context. His disciples had been arguing which of them would be greatest in His coming kingdom. Like kids at an ice cream truck, they all wanted to be first. Jesus, however, informed them that if they *truly* wanted to be first, they must put themselves last in their lives. It depended on how badly they wanted exalted positions in heaven. If they served others, God would see to it that they were rewarded beyond measure. But if they didn't want to pay such a price, they'd still go to heaven; they just wouldn't be as greatly rewarded. There was no compulsion. It was up to them. Christ commanded, "Store up for yourselves treasures in heaven" (Matthew 6:20 NIV), and then told them a surefire way to obtain that treasure. The question is: How badly do you want eternal rewards?

Father, You sent Your own Son in the form of a servant to save us.
And You exalted Him to Your right hand and made His name
above all others. You reward Your servants—help us to look to
You for our reward and joyfully take on the role of a servant.

Refusing to Complain

Do not say, "Why were the old days better than these?"
For it is not wise to ask such questions.
ECCLESIASTES 7:10 NIV

• •

Many older men can remember when the economy was in a steady upward climb and financial stability was the norm. Middle-aged men miss the years before the Great Recession when they could take job security for granted. Young men were just entering the labor pool when the global downturn hit and all the rules changed. And everyone has the tendency to ask, "Why were the old days better than these?"

While this may be a natural question, the Bible says it's not wise to look at life that way, because basically it's just a complaint. It's a lack of trusting God. Now, this is not to make light of the situation you face. Times are difficult, and for you they may be very difficult. Career and work issues attack a man's self-esteem. Having a family who looks to you for leadership and provision raises the stakes even higher. But complaining won't make things better. It will only contribute to defeat.

Instead, you must "gird up the loins of your mind" (1 Peter 1:13 NKJV) and refuse to give in to despair. If beans and rice are the new normal, you must learn to make the most of them, knowing that hard times won't last forever. In the meantime, you can say with Paul, "I have learned the secret of being content in any and every situation. . .whether living in plenty or in want" (Philippians 4:12 NIV). Having a satisfied mind and refusing to give up leads to victory.

God, I have so often looked back and wished for past days!
Forgive me for not staying current with You and what You are
trying to teach me. Help me to trust in You no matter what the
circumstances are, and to become a better son in the process.

Valentine's Day

*Many waters cannot quench love; rivers cannot sweep
it away. If one were to give all the wealth of one's
house for love, it would be utterly scorned.*
SONG OF SONGS 8:7 NIV

• •

Saint Valentine's Day began as a feast day for a Christian martyr named Valentinus—in English, Valentine. According to one legend, while Valentine was in prison, he healed the daughter of his jailer. Then, just before his execution, he wrote her a letter and closed with the words, "Your Valentine." During the late Middle Ages, this day became associated with romantic love, and in later centuries lovers began giving each other flowers, candy, and Valentine cards. Soon these cards were decorated with baby Cupids shooting arrows, shared from kindergarten to retirement homes.

Many people are enthralled with the idea of romantic love, and it's the theme of the majority of pop songs. They think that the euphoric feeling of "being in love" is the ultimate human experience. It is pleasant, but it's only the effect of a few cents' worth of the love chemical serotonin coursing through their brains. Serotonin is responsible for feelings of infatuation and obsessing over someone. After this initial "in love" stage, however, a chemical called oxytocin is responsible for a desire for long-term attachment. Many people go through life constantly falling in and out of "love," pursuing emotional rushes from new serotonin surges. But marriages need unselfish love if they are to survive. Only then will love be strong enough so that waters of emotional storms cannot quench it and rivers of hard times cannot sweep it away.

*Father of love, You created marriage and all the romantic
feelings that go with it. But real love was demonstrated in the
unselfish life and sacrifice of Your Son. Help us as husbands,
and fathers, to live as servants to our families and the world.*

Shameless Persistence

*"But I tell you this—though he won't do it for friendship's sake,
if you keep knocking long enough, he will get up and give you
whatever you need because of your shameless persistence."*
LUKE 11:8 NLT

. . . .

Jesus told a story about a man whose friend arrived at his house at midnight. The friend was famished, but the man had nothing to feed him. But he remembered that his neighbor had some bread. So he ran to his neighbor's house, beat on his door, and shouted till he woke him up. His neighbor crossly replied that the door was locked and he was in bed, so he wasn't about to get up and give him anything. The fact that they were friends made no difference. But Jesus pointed out that if the man refused to take no for an answer and continued pounding and calling, the neighbor *would* finally get up and give him bread. This was shameless audacity at its finest. Jesus then applied this lesson to prayer: "And so I tell you, keep on asking, and you will receive what you ask for" (verse 9). Now, don't miss the point: God isn't a grumpy neighbor who must be pestered before He begrudgingly answers. Jesus was emphasizing the importance of persistence. State your request and state it again—and again and again the way your kids do when they really want something! Some people think that repeating a request shows a lack of faith, but you can be sure that the man *knew* that if he kept knocking long enough, he'd be given what he was asking for. So be shamelessly persistent—maybe even a little childish!

*God my Father, help me to learn persistence in prayer. I want
to show You that I believe by not giving up. Please hear my prayers
and answer! And in the waiting, teach me how to be at peace,
without quitting or accusing You of not caring.*

Uncertain Wealth

*Will you set your eyes on that which is not? For riches certainly make
themselves wings; they fly away like an eagle toward heaven.*
PROVERBS 23:5 NKJV

• •

Riches are "that which is not." They appear to be solid but can quickly
come to nothing. In other words, as solid and enduring as an ounce of
gold might seem, it's more like a drop of water dancing in a hot frying
pan, getting smaller and smaller until it finally sizzles into nothingness.
Those who work in the stock market see this often. Most men, in fact,
have experienced enough financial setbacks to testify to the truth of
this principle. And there's no dad in the whole world who hasn't seen
his paycheck eaten up by unexpected doctor's visits, school expenses,
wrecked cars, prom dresses—the list is endless!

Even if you manage to frugally sock away vast riches in a secure
savings account where they steadily increase, you will *still* be separated
from your wealth. . .guaranteed! "The hot sun rises and the grass withers;
the little flower droops and falls, and its beauty fades away. In the same
way, the rich will fade away" (James 1:11 NLT).

So the Bible warns: "If riches increase, do not set your heart on
them" (Psalm 62:10 NKJV). Riches can decrease just as quickly as they
increased—and even if they don't, you yourself will fly away toward
heaven, an eternal realm where temporal riches mean nothing at all. So
Paul advises believers not to trust in their money "which is so unreliable,"
and adds, "Their trust should be in God, who richly gives us all we need"
(1 Timothy 6:17 NLT). Certainly you should set aside funds for emergencies
and retirement, handling your income as a faithful steward, but ultimately
your trust must be in God, who does not change or disappear.

*God of all wealth, we praise You for Your constant supply of love
and hope and forgiveness. Help us to keep money in its place—as a
servant of Your kingdom, helping the needs of those around us.*

Regular Spiritual Checkups

But exhort one another daily, while it is called "Today,"
lest any of you be hardened through the deceitfulness of sin.
HEBREWS 3:13 NKJV

• •

No kid ever loved going to the doctor. Probably because there's always a possibility of getting a shot! Some grown men are still kids in this respect, stubbornly refusing to go see a doctor and get a checkup even when they're in pain or have had symptoms for some time. They figure they'll just tough it out. After all, going to the doctor takes time—time they can't afford. Or maybe they don't want to hear they should change their eating or drinking habits or some other lifestyle choice. So they persuade themselves that it's nothing and that it will eventually go away of its own accord. Whatever their reasons, many men put off getting a checkup long after they know something's not right.

Some guys treat their spiritual health the same way. God knows the way men reason. He also knows that sin is deceitful. It often begins as an innocent thought, which leads into a not-so-harmless thought, which leads to temptation, which leads to sin. Being tricked into sinning once is bad enough, but when a man frequently gives in to the same vice, over time it hardens into an entrenched habit, not easily rooted out. You may have a particular besetting sin, "the sin which so easily ensnares [you]" (Hebrews 12:1 NKJV)—and there are many sins that are common to men. That's why God counsels men to "exhort one another daily. . . lest any of you be hardened through the deceitfulness of sin." If you're struggling with a stubborn sin, make yourself accountable to a solid, trusted Christian friend. Then follow up. Go for your spiritual checkup faithfully. You'll be glad you did.

God, You know our inner thoughts and our deepest emotions. You alone are able to heal us, but only if we submit to You as the Great Physician.

Power over Enemies

*Though they plot evil against you and devise
wicked schemes, they cannot succeed.*
PSALM 21:11 NIV

• •

Paul asks, "If God is for us, who can be against us?" (Romans 8:31 NIV).
In a glum moment you might answer, "*Lots* of people." And that's true.
Lots of people could set themselves against you. We learn this from our
earliest days on the playground. Bullies, cliques, other kids who want
your place in line—it's a pattern of human nature. Enemies are easy to
collect even for decent folks!

When you read the Psalms you see that David was constantly praying
for God to deliver him from new enemies. But the question is: Who can
effectively oppose you? Who can prevail over you? Isaiah wrote, "'Those
who contend with you will be as nothing and will perish. You will seek
those who quarrel with you, but will not find them, those who war with
you will be as nothing and non-existent'" (Isaiah 41:11–12 NASB). If you're
God's child, doing His will and seeking to please Him, your enemies
can't succeed. They may utter fearful threats and seem to succeed for
a time, but God is on your side. You will prevail. As Romans 8:32–35
says, if God didn't keep back His own Son but sent Him to die for you,
won't He also freely give you all things, including protection? So what if
your enemies bring charges against you? God is the one who justifies,
and He's on your side. So what if men condemn you? Jesus Christ is at
God's right hand. He loves you and is interceding for you. And who can
separate you from this great love? No one. Trust God, stay close to Him
in the Secret Place of the Most High, and He will protect you.

*Father, if our hope is not in You, then whom can we ever turn to?
And if our hope is in You, then who can ever succeed in
opposing us? We have life eternal and Your Spirit for today.*

Gentle Men of God

*But we were gentle among you, just as a nursing mother cherishes
her own children. . . . We exhorted, and comforted, and charged
every one of you, as a father does his own children.*
1 THESSALONIANS 2:7, 11 NKJV

• •

There could hardly be a more perfect picture of gentleness than a nursing mother tenderly cradling a newborn infant in her arms as she nurses him, lovingly cherishing him. No sudden movements, no loud sounds. Only soft words and tender care. The apostle Paul said this is how he acted toward the Christians of Thessalonica. He went on to say that he had comforted and taught them like a loving father does his own children. Picture a father hugging and reassuring a small child, wiping away her tears. Elsewhere Paul wrote that "a servant of the Lord must not quarrel but be gentle to all" (2 Timothy 2:24 NKJV). You are to be gentle to others, even when correcting them, starting with your own family.

Men are commonly referred to as "gentlemen," and you may think a gentleman is simply an old-fashioned title. But a gentleman is exactly that—a *gentle man*. God is a gentle Father, and you should be, too. If you want to be truly great, remember that greatness doesn't come from bossing people around or snapping your fingers and expecting them to jump, but by gently instructing them. David said to God, "Your gentleness makes me great" (Psalm 18:35 NASB).

*Gentle Father, open my eyes to the ways I've been harsh with
my children, impatient with my wife, and rough with others.
It's so easy as I push through my day to run over those I care about!
Help me to see where gentleness can be glorifying to You.*

No Bad Loans

*One who is gracious to a poor man lends to the L*ORD*,
and He will repay him for his good deed.*
PROVERBS 19:17 NASB

• •

While the concept of God borrowing money may seem odd, it's actually scriptural. When you give to the poor, the Bible says you're lending to the Lord. Now, God sometimes does outright miracles to provide money, but more often He wants to involve His children. He wants you to experience the joy of giving. So frequently God chooses to borrow cash from people like you. He will then see to it that you're repaid! And the good news is that God always comes through with His repayments. He never forgets. There are never "insufficient funds" in His bank account, so it's no risk to make Him a loan.

Happily, you don't need to give begrudgingly, wondering if that's the last you'll see of your hard-earned cash. God says, "Give generously to them and do so without a grudging heart; then because of this the LORD your God will bless you in all your work and in everything you put your hand to" (Deuteronomy 15:10 NIV). That's something else: God doesn't always repay in the same currency He borrows. Many times He's very creative. But He will never shortchange you. He will always repay with interest—whether in this life or in the next.

This is a lesson we fathers can pass on to our kids only by setting the example. Generosity is part of the legacy God has always planned for His people. So be glad when God comes along looking for a loan. And yes, while it's true that you must also exercise wisdom and not simply give to everyone looking for a handout, God calls His children to be generous.

Father, You alone provide for us, and we can please You by being as generous toward those in need as You are to us. Thank You for being involved in our giving so that we know it is never wasted.

The Source of Power

The LORD is the everlasting God, the Creator of all the earth.
He never grows weak or weary. . . . He gives power
to the weak and strength to the powerless.
ISAIAH 40:28–29 NLT

• •

God has absolutely unlimited power. He created the earth and the entire universe full of billions and trillions of stars, but this astonishing feat didn't tucker Him out. It didn't leave Him weak and weary.

God has unlimited power to this day and still delights in doing the miraculous. Human beings, however, have definite limitations to their strength. A hard day's work wipes us out. A ten-minute run wearies us. A stressful day can leave us mentally exhausted. And kids were designed to show us our limitations! But after saying the above, Isaiah went on to explain, "Those who trust in the LORD will find new strength" (verse 31). God can empower you when your batteries are running low. In fact, even if you suffer from permanent disabilities and limitations, God can infuse you with His strength and help you accomplish things that you could never accomplish even if you had full health and strength.

Once when the apostle Paul was asking God to heal a medical condition, God told him, "My grace is all you need. My power works best in weakness" (2 Corinthians 12:9 NLT). This totally changed Paul's thinking, and he concluded, "I take pleasure in my weaknesses. . . . For when I am weak, then I am strong" (verse 10). You don't necessarily *feel* strong when you have God's strength working through you, but you are strong.

Powerful Father, You are the source of our strength, our energy, and
our hope! You alone can give us the power to carry on the work You've
assigned us in this world. Help us to remember You in the rush of life—
that You designed us to need Your refreshing!

Clothed with Humility

Likewise you younger people, submit yourselves to your elders.
Yes, all of you be submissive to one another,
and be clothed with humility.
1 PETER 5:5 NKJV

. . . .

It's a sign of a good upbringing to respect your elders. For Peter, it was a reasonable request to ask young men to submit to their elders. But Christianity goes further. Jesus wants you to respect others, regardless of their age. That means that old men must also honor young men, listen to them, and follow their advice. . .if it's sound. To do that takes great humility. You have to be secure in your manhood to submit to someone much younger than yourself. It takes a self-effacing attitude to let others have their way when you could demand to be considered first.

The expression "be clothed with humility" brings this out. When you get dressed in the morning, you choose your clothes according to what you'll be doing. If you'll be lounging around the house, you wear casual clothes. If you'll be attending a formal event, you dress up. If you'll be changing the oil in your car, you pick your grubbiest work clothes. To clothe yourself with humility means to make a conscious decision that you're not going to insist on *your* way but are determined to put others first. Elsewhere Paul advised, "Let nothing be done through selfish ambition or conceit, but in lowliness of mind let each esteem others better than himself" (Philippians 2:3 NKJV). He wasn't suggesting that you nurture an inferiority complex. He was talking about having humility.

Father, how hard it is for me to be humble on any regular basis. Getting humbled is one thing, but choosing humility as a mindset is something else all together! Help me to clothe myself in the attitude of Christ, making myself a servant to those You've placed in my life.

Learning What Works

Paul and his friends went through Phrygia and Galatia, but the Holy Spirit would not let them preach in Asia. After they arrived in Mysia, they tried to go into Bithynia, but the Spirit of Jesus would not let them.
ACTS 16:6–7 CEV

• •

It takes a tremendous amount of faith and courage to try to start a new business, because according to studies, eight out of ten entrepreneurs crash within eighteen months. Fully 80 percent of new businesses are doomed to fail.

You know the challenges if you've ever attempted to start anything bigger than a lemonade stand. (And even those can be tough!) You start out with high hopes, certain that you're going to beat the odds because you have such a good idea, such a great product, and such a catchy business name. Plus, you reason, God is on your side, so you're *sure* to succeed. But in the Bible, even godly men trying their best to be about God's business had a hard time figuring out where to go and when to go there.

Paul and his team went through Phrygia and Galatia seeking an opportunity, but God blocked them. Perplexed and perhaps frustrated, they tried to launch into Bithynia. Again they were blocked. And they couldn't blame it on a dip in the economy, poor financing, or a bad business location. God Himself was preventing them from succeeding. So they just kept trying and kept seeking God, until He opened a door in Greece. We need that kind of humble perseverance for our own growth, but our kids need to see it in action just as much.

So don't give up! Sometimes you just have to keep seeking and keep praying for God to open the door *He* wants you to go through.

*Father, sometimes You frustrate our plans so we keep
seeking You and move toward areas we might not have.
Give us the patience to persevere and trust in You!*

Patient in Everything

In everything we do, we show that we are true ministers of God.
We patiently endure troubles and hardships and calamities of every kind.
2 CORINTHIANS 6:4 NLT

• •

Any man can cheerfully follow God when everything is going fine. But the true measure of a man is how he holds up when troubles and hardships arise, especially those that last for prolonged periods of time. Do you complain to those around you, or lose your temper, or become impatient with your family? Or do you seek God all the more? It takes patience to endure, trusting that if you give it a little more time, God will work things out.

But the ultimate test for a man comes when calamities strike. It's a calamity when an economic downturn hits, wiping out months of carefully managed savings. It's a calamity when once-reliable markets dry up, causing business losses, layoffs, and financial insecurity. It's a calamity when a traffic collision or a workplace accident leaves you injured and unable to work. It's hard for any man, but hardest for fathers who watch the impact it has on their families.

Do not be the "strong, silent type"! Give voice to your troubles by pouring out your complaints to God as King David did in the Psalms; share your woes with those who can give you wise counsel, but above all protect your children by finding someone to share your feelings with rather than burdening them. If God is taking you through harsh times, it's to make you more like His Son. Trust in Him as your Father, and know He is with you.

Father! How little I know of real faith, real patience, real love! If You test me with hardship, teach me to accept it as a gift. I want to be an authentic son, and what You have called me to suffer, let it do Your work in me.

Reasonable Expectations

"Some of the children are very young, and the flocks and herds have their young, too. If they are driven too hard, even for one day, all the animals could die. . . . We will follow slowly, at a pace that is comfortable for the livestock and the children."
GENESIS 33:13–14 NLT

• •

When Jacob and his family and all his flocks and herds arrived in Canaan, Esau and four hundred men came galloping up from Edom to meet them. Esau was then bound and determined that his brother should move to Edom with him—and right now. After all, his four hundred men were eager to get back to their own flocks. But Jacob explained that it would be detrimental to drive too hard. He needed to move at a reasonable pace. He was a father, and he knew what his children could and could not handle.

It's easier to temper expectations of your children when they come from someone else. But what about the ones we have of them? Perhaps you excelled in certain chores, subjects, or sports as a child and feel that if *you* could do it, they should be able to as well. Now, fathers have the right to expect certain behavior from their children, but they need to guard against unreasonable expectations. These will either anger their children or discourage them. Paul cautioned, "Fathers, do not provoke your children to anger" (Ephesians 6:4 NASB), and elsewhere wrote, "Fathers, do not exasperate your children, so that they will not lose heart" (Colossians 3:21 NASB). Yes, at times children need to be pushed gently beyond their perceived limits, but first know them well, and set the bar accordingly. They'll be happy if they're able to please you, and you'll be happy to watch them grow.

*Father in heaven, help us as fathers to know
our children well, and do the same for them.*

Resting in God

"Be still, and know that I am God; I will be exalted
among the nations, I will be exalted in the earth."
PSALM 46:10 NIV

• •

Whether you celebrate Saturday or Sunday as the Sabbath, it's important to take one day of rest a week. It was a principle so important, it was a commandment in the Old Testament: "Six days you shall labor and do all your work, but the seventh day is a Sabbath to the LORD your God. On it you shall not do any work" (Exodus 20:9-10 NIV).

God knew—and science has since discovered—that your body needs to take a break once a week. So take a day to relax and recharge your batteries. But the purpose of the Sabbath is not merely to rest physically. By ceasing your own efforts, deliberately slowing down and focusing on God, you show that you trust Him with your entire life. In that sense, you should enter a "Sabbath rest" every day. That's why the Lord says, "Be still, and know that I am God." Or as the New American Standard Bible puts it, "Cease striving and know that I am God."

Certainly God expects you to work hard to provide for your family. But He also wants you to realize that "it is *He* who gives you power to get wealth" (Deuteronomy 8:18 NKJV, emphasis added). He's the one who blessed you with a family, who protects you, watches over you, and cares for you in every way. So throughout the week—and especially on the Sabbath—have a trusting attitude, spend time in the Word and in prayer, and remind yourself that God is in charge.

Good Father, let us rest in You and in Your great finished work of
salvation. You remember us, how we are made of clay and dust,
and You know we need refreshing. Thank You for being our
shield and protector, our rest and our refreshment.

Following Godly Mentors

Remember those who led you, who spoke the word of God to you; and considering the result of their conduct, imitate their faith.
HEBREWS 13:7 NASB

• •

Western society puts great emphasis on being an independent, self-made man—being one's own boss—and it's true that you must be able to stand on your own two feet and make your own way in this world. But there's also tremendous value in recognizing the authority of pastors and spiritual leaders. There's great wisdom in seeking the counsel of senior saints who have walked the walk for many years and have much to teach. Consider "the result of their conduct"—the good fruit of a sincere Christian lifestyle, and the wisdom that comes with years of serving the Lord and studying His Word.

It's wise to submit to spiritual leadership, just as it's wise for your children to submit to your guidance. Some men might resist the idea of being mentored, especially as they get older. But you're never too old to learn. If you live to be one hundred, wouldn't you still be happy to have your seventy-five-year-old son ask for your advice?

Paul said, "Let all who are spiritually mature agree on these things. If you disagree on some point, I believe God will make it plain to you" (Philippians 3:15 NLT). So don't be afraid to follow the counsel of spiritual leaders and emulate the lifestyle of godly mentors. It's wise to seek out good role models, and it's wise to be teachable.

God our Father, You are the teacher of all things by Your Holy Spirit. Thank You that You have raised up fathers, mentors, teachers, counselors, and guides among Your people to help us grow in pleasing You.

Put Your Trust in God

*Trust in the LORD with all your heart and lean not on
your own understanding; in all your ways submit to him,
and he will make your paths straight.*
PROVERBS 3:5–6 NIV

. . . .

No matter your level of education, you don't have all the answers to whatever life throws at you. Heck, by the time our kids know how to ask questions we begin to realize how little we know!

Whether it's a difficult predicament, an unexpected turn of events, or a tragic loss, you may find yourself struggling to solve a problem and unable to explain why something negative has happened. God has all the answers. You don't need to look any further or seek comfort from anyone else. He has your best interest at heart. He knows what you need. All you have to do is submit to Him, praise Him for the successes in your life, and turn to Him at times of hardship. The Lord will guide you through every situation no matter the circumstances. But you must ask Him to direct you, and you must seek God's will in everything you do. Turn every area of your life over to Him. There's no halfway with God. You can't choose to follow Him some of the time and ignore Him other times.

If you make your heavenly Father a vital part of everything you do, He will lead you because He wants His children to grow into the image of Jesus. God knows what is best for you. He is a better judge of what you need than you are, so you must trust Him completely in every choice you make.

*Trustworthy Father, help me to lean on You rather than on my own
understanding or my own resources. I get impatient for answers,
Father, and sometimes I look for solutions that don't put You first.
Forgive me and teach me to wait upon You.*

It's All Good

And we know that in all things God works for the good of those
who love him, who have been called according to his purpose.
ROMANS 8:28 NIV

• •

God works in everything for our good. He doesn't pick and choose situations. He doesn't care about us only on certain days. He loves us every second of every minute of every hour of every day.

We may face hardships. We may have people speaking ill about us. We may endure unbearable physical or emotional suffering. We may watch our children go through unbearable circumstances. But even in the "worst" situations, God is committed to our long-term betterment. He is always working to conform us, and our children, into the image of His Son.

God makes this promise not to everyone, but to those who are filled by the Holy Spirit, those who love Him, those who put Him first in their lives, those who don't care about worldly treasures, and those who determine heaven is their first priority. If you love God with all your heart, soul, and mind and live your daily life acting out this unconditional love through your interactions with others, He will take care of the rest for you and your family. All you have to do is believe in Him, exercise your faith, and work toward building His kingdom.

Father, how loving and kind You are to allow us to become Your
children! And how committed You are to our maturity in Christ to bear
with us through every hardship that will make us more like Him. Give us
the patience and faith to see Your kingdom forged in all circumstances.

To God Be the Glory

Humble yourselves, therefore, under God's mighty hand,
that he may lift you up in due time.
1 PETER 5:6 NIV

- -

From our first steps as a baby, we learn to love the praise of our parents. It's supposed to be that way. But as we get older we begin to seek other sources of approval—some legitimate, some not. It's easy to take credit for our success and accomplishments when we did all the hard work. We put in long hours studying when in school and made many sacrifices along the way to earn that diploma. We worked tirelessly at a job and spent the extra effort to prove ourselves worthy of that promotion. So it's no wonder we soak in all the praise when everything pays off.

But, what about Dad? Remember Him? He created us and blessed us with the gifts we needed to get excellent grades, to work diligently, and to achieve great things. He put us in position to be right where we are at this moment. Have we thanked Him today? Have we given Him the credit? Is He the one who really matters as we take these next steps?

Let us humble ourselves, exalt Him, and tell others about the wonders He has done in our lives. Don't waste time worrying about social standing, position on the corporate ladder, and status. Replace the praise of others with the praise of a happy Father. His recognition is more important than what anyone else thinks of us. He will bless us far more than we can imagine. He is a good, good Father.

I love to see You happy, Father! I want to humble myself right now
and take one more baby step toward You. There's nothing I can do on
this earth apart from You that would bring You joy, but in Your Spirit,
I know I can delight You, my good, good Father.

Help One Another

*"The King will reply, 'Truly I tell you, whatever you did for one
of the least of these brothers and sisters of mine, you did for me.'"*
MATTHEW 25:40 NIV

• •

Have you ever passed a homeless person on the street corner and looked away, avoiding eye contact? Have you continued on your way instead of offering help—food, drink, clothing, shelter, or money? Would you ignore that person if it were your own child? If it were Jesus Himself standing right before you? Certainly, you wouldn't.

Look for opportunities to extend a hand to someone in need. Jesus specifically says that whatever you do for someone else you do for Him, especially the weak and downcast. Whether you give food or clothes to the homeless, visit someone in prison, serve in a shelter, or look after someone who is sick, you are giving to the Lord. He's watching you. Be thankful for all your blessings and be mindful that others may not be so fortunate. Don't take what you have for granted. Share what God has given you with someone who has less than you, and teach your children to do the same. Perhaps you don't have much to give in the way of food or money or clothing. But it doesn't cost anything to go see an elderly person and lend a listening ear. It's free to visit someone in prison and offer a word of encouragement. The Lord Himself waits somewhere—on the street, in a nursing home, in a hospital bed—for all of us to find Him.

*Lord Jesus, You are all around me in the situations of other people.
You give me more opportunities to serve You than I could ever
imagine—but I often overlook them, and You in the process.
Lord, help me to see You when I see the needs around me.*

Careful What You Say

"But I say, if you are even angry with someone, you are subject to judgment! If you call someone an idiot, you are in danger of being brought before the court. And if you curse someone, you are in danger of the fires of hell."
MATTHEW 5:22 NLT

. . . .

Everyone knows murder is wrong. It's against the law and breaks the fifth commandment. Thankfully, it's not an everyday event for most communities. But Jesus points to the root of the issue, which is a pretty common problem: anger. It's a strong, possibly dangerous emotion. We see it manifest itself from the earliest days of life, and as parents we know how much damage it can do if left uncontrolled—bitterness, emotional pain, mental anguish, and spiritual damage.

Jesus was pointing out that you don't have to go all the way to murder to have sinned—simply being angry with someone goes against God's commandment to love one another. And, if uncontrolled, will prevent you from developing a closer relationship with God. When you express selfish anger, you are moving away from the example He set for you in the way He lived His life. Jesus didn't fight back when the soldiers crucified Him. He didn't curse at them or raise His voice in anger.

When someone makes you mad, rather than retaliating with hurtful words or physical violence, remember how Jesus responded to His critics and the men who put Him on the cross. Exercise self-control and try to respond in a manner that would please God. He will hold you accountable for your attitude, so train yourself to control your thoughts, and that will make it easier for you to show restraint and avoid anger.

Father of peace, I know from experience how easily I can become angry. . .it takes so little to set me off! Help me to cultivate a quiet spirit before You.

Walk Your Talk

*"Prove by the way you live that you have
repented of your sins and turned to God."*
MATTHEW 3:8 NLT

• •

Some Jewish leaders followed the Old Testament laws and oral traditions passed down for generations. John the Baptist criticized these leaders, calling them hypocrites for being too legalistic, and he accused them of using religion to advance their political power. John the Baptist challenged them to change their behavior and prove through their actions and by the way they lived their lives—not through words or rituals—that they had turned to God.

You've heard these sayings: "Practice what you preach" and "Actions speak louder than words." As a dad you may have even said something like this to your kids to emphasize the importance of integrity.

When we look to ourselves, are we being consistent? You may say that you're a Christian. You read the Bible. You go to church. You offer tithes. Is it because you are following the rules in your particular denomination? Is it because you were raised that way? Or do you truly practice what you preach from a changed heart? Do you walk your Christian talk? Do others see Christ in you in your daily life, and words and activities? Is it from the heart that you do what you do for God?

Only you and God know the answer to these important questions. God knows your true heart and intentions. He looks beyond all religious practices and ultimately will judge everyone based on the heart. If Jesus is King of your heart, your walk will match your talk.

Father, You want us to do good and to act like Christ, but we can't do it without truly relying on Him. Help us to examine our ways to put everything under His control, so that we don't fall into the trap of the Pharisees. We want our lives to be the result of a changed heart.

Give Me Strength

I can do all things through Christ who strengthens me.
PHILIPPIANS 4:13 NKJV

• •

The apostle Paul turned to Christianity after condemning and even murdering Christians. He eventually dedicated his life to serving Christ, and his journey led him to abundant provision, extreme poverty, and everything in between. He was shipwrecked three times but still used it to accomplish his mission. He was imprisoned for several years but still wrote this joyful letter from prison. When Paul says he "can do all things through Christ," he's not talking about superhuman ability to accomplish goals that satisfy his own purposes. Paul learned to get by with whatever he had, whether it was little or nothing, and wherever he found himself, planned or unplanned. His focus remained the same—preaching the good news of Jesus Christ. Paul set his priorities in order and was grateful for all that God gave him. Paul faced many trials and tribulations, but he found joy in serving the Lord and was not deterred by any trouble he encountered along the way.

Paul's lesson is one for us to learn, too, and to pass on. It's a process that takes one step at a time, but you will never be alone in that process. As Paul so confidently asserts: You also "can do all things *through Christ*." You can accomplish any task, overcome any adversity, and survive any trouble if you come to the Lord and ask Him to strengthen you. He will not grant you the power to accomplish anything that does not serve His interests, but He will help you every step of the way as you build your faith and develop a relationship with Him.

God of all circumstances, help me to lean on You in trouble and in success. Give me the strength to continue on, serving, caring, trusting in all situations. Let me lead my family with the peace that comes from knowing Christ is my strength.

Forgive Me, Father

Restore to me the joy of your salvation, and make me willing to obey you. Then I will teach your ways to rebels, and they will return to you.
PSALM 51:12–13 NLT

• •

Have you ever caught one of your kids trying to hide their wrongdoing? Have you ever heard the excuse that they were afraid of what you might think or do? Remember the feeling of distance that fear created and how much you wanted the closeness of your relationship restored?

Have *you* ever felt disconnected from God because of your sin? Perhaps you are so embarrassed by *your* actions that you feel unworthy of being in the Lord's presence. King David felt this way when he sinned with Bathsheba. In his prayer, he cries out to God: "Restore to me the joy of your salvation." David truly repented of his sin and asked for forgiveness; he longed for the closeness to be restored

God wants you to be close to Him, but sin drives a wedge between you and Him. Unconfessed sin pushes you further away from God, if you don't confront it, ask Him for forgiveness, and learn to obey Him. Even then, you may end up suffering earthly consequences for your sin. For example, adultery may lead to divorce. Fraud may lead to imprisonment. But God's forgiveness gives you the joy of a relationship with Him regardless of any other consequences

Once you experience that joy, like David, you will want to share it with others. David wanted to teach "rebels" and help them "return" to the Lord. You can help your friends and relatives by telling them about the joy of God's forgiveness and your fellowship with Him.

Good and loving Father, You always seek us out when we sin. You want closeness; You want fellowship; You want intimacy! Thank You for pursuing us and not allowing us to stay estranged from You.

Critical Self-Analysis

I realize how kind God has been to me, and so I tell each of you not to think you are better than you really are. Use good sense and measure yourself by the amount of faith that God has given you.
ROMANS 12:3 CEV

• •

It's important to have self-esteem and healthy confidence in the talents, skills, and abilities God has given you. As fathers, we work to instill those values in our children—literally for years!

However, none of us should overestimate our worth by basing our evaluation of ourselves on worldly standards. The true measure of your worth to the Lord isn't found in your bank statements, your job title, the size of your house, or the cost of your luxury vehicle. You must be honest and accurate in your self-evaluation, ignoring the world's standards of success and achievement. You are esteemed by God for the amount of faith that you have, not the total sum of your material possessions. All that you have is a gift from God. Recognizing, acknowledging, and being grateful for His blessings will keep you from becoming prideful, arrogant, or conceited in your success in this life. It will lead you into true humility because whatever you are, God made you so. He wants you to use the gifts He's given you rather than waste them, but He wants you to understand and appreciate why you have those skills. Tools from God are meant to be used for building His kingdom and not our own.

Father in heaven, You alone have equipped us with talents, gifts, and abilities, as well as the opportunity to use them. You have good works for us to do so that we grow in the character of Your Son, Jesus. Remind us daily that we can only be pleasing to You by using our gifts in faith.

Be a Voice for the Voiceless

*Speak up for those who cannot speak for themselves;
ensure justice for those being crushed. Yes, speak up for
the poor and helpless, and see that they get justice.*
PROVERBS 31:8–9 NLT

• •

There are instances when you find yourself with information about a situation that can help or hurt someone's character or career. Perhaps you overheard a story or someone shared something with you that you didn't even want to know. It is important to remember that you always have to speak the truth. God doesn't want His children taking sides. You have to stand up for what is right no matter the repercussions.

Speak up for those who can't speak up for themselves. If you see someone being bullied, help them. Make it clear to the bully that their behavior is wrong. Children are another example. They can't defend themselves, and they often seek help from their parents. You should always remember to ask your children about their day, ask about what happened at school and how people treated them. You have to look out for them and always put their best interest first. Always remind your children that you are there for them and you will protect them just like your heavenly Father does for you.

*Thank You, Father in heaven, for standing up for us in Christ!
Help us to stand up for the helpless as Jesus did. Give us courage
to stand for what is right regardless of the consequences,
knowing You are the only one we need to please.*

Lead by Example

Direct your children onto the right path,
and when they are older, they will not leave it.
PROVERBS 22:6 NLT

• •

Children are a precious gift from God, a blessing greater than any other. It's your responsibility as a parent to raise your children to know God, to love Him, and to fear Him. Teach them to glorify His name in their thoughts, in their words, and in their actions. But you must set the example yourself! Show them by your example and they will learn to follow your path.

Raising children in a healthy church, teaching them the scriptures from an early age, and impressing upon them the joy of a relationship with Christ will set a foundation for life that supports your example.

Another essential part of putting your kids on the right path is allowing them to make decisions for themselves. They need to stand on their own, recognize right from wrong, and learn to acknowledge the Lord for themselves. As they are able, encourage them to make decisions and discuss how those choices can please the Lord. Don't shelter them from the consequences either—they need to know early on that even if following the Lord is tough, He will bless them with a deeper understanding of His will. Ultimately, the reason they won't leave the path is because they have come to acknowledge Him as their eternal Father.

Eternal God, my Father, thank You for giving us the
right path in Your Son! Help me to put my children on
this right path, to please You, their one true Father.

Train Your Soul

*Have nothing to do with godless myths and old wives' tales;
rather, train yourself to be godly. For physical training
is of some value, but godliness has value for all things,
holding promise for both the present life and the life to come.*
1 TIMOTHY 4:7–8 NIV

. . . .

Our society puts a lot of emphasis on the outward appearance, especially for the young. With the billions spent on marketing aimed at kids, the invention of the selfie, and the constant barrage of images from television and the Internet, young people are pushed to think about appearance day and night. There's nothing wrong with eating healthy food, exercising, and doing whatever you can to ensure you look your best—within reason. But there's so much emphasis placed on looks that it can become depressing trying to keep up—especially as you get older!

But are you in shape spiritually as well as physically? Your spiritual health is far more important because the results of it last forever. Your physical health can and will fail at some point, but your spiritual health will sustain you. It will carry you through the difficult times; it will help you endure tragedy and hardship. Physical health is a real blessing, but your spiritual well-being will benefit you the most in the long run. So, before you go to the gym, make sure you haven't neglected your spiritual muscles! Use the abilities God has given you to help others around you, to share His love, and to praise Him with all your heart, mind, and strength.

*God of power and strength, we praise You for spiritual health
and for physical health. But we know which one lasts and
which one doesn't. Train us spiritually! Teach us to exercise
our spiritual muscles in service to Your unending kingdom.*

Be Strong in Suffering

That is why we never give up. Though our bodies are dying,
our spirits are being renewed every day. For our present
troubles are small and won't last very long. Yet they produce
for us a glory that vastly outweighs them and will last forever!
2 CORINTHIANS 4:16–17 NLT

• •

Whenever you face tough problems at work, struggle with disobedience in your kids, or face conflict with your wife, it's easy to want to quit. Paul faced daily struggles and persecution that wore him down. But even when he was sent to prison, Paul never gave up on his goal to spread the good news. No matter the hardships you face, the pain or anger, the fatigue or criticism, focus on gaining inner strength from the Holy Spirit and continue to push forward. The people who frustrate you need you to persevere; you are serving them though it doesn't seem like it at the time. And, you have an eternal reward waiting for you! So take courage, and don't give it up because you're feeling the pressure today. Commit yourself to serving the Lord and He will empower you, turning your weakness into strength. Don't allow your troubles to diminish your faith, but look for how God is using them to strengthen it. There *is* purpose in your suffering, even though you may never understand it. God can show His power through you. Your problems are opportunities for Him to work through you and for you to witness for Him.

Father of our faith, strengthen us in all our times of testing!
We don't always recognize Your hand in conflict or hardship,
but You are there with us, using all circumstances for our good.

Whose Fool Are You?

The fool says in his heart, "There is no God."
PSALM 53:1 ESV

• •

April Fools' Day is a time for innocent pranks, harmless deceptions, and entertaining practical jokes. But being foolish in our lives and decisions isn't a laughing matter. Most of the misery we experience in life is the result of the foolish choices we, or others, make.

The Bible is clear. Those who reject God and the truth of His Word are foolish. But the world regards those who love God and live by His Word as foolish (1 Corinthians 1:27). It seems the real question isn't whether or not someone will think we are foolish, but whose judgment we value. This is the lesson most needed by our children to make good decisions over a lifetime.

Those who reject God and His wisdom are certain they are wise and believers are foolish. They point to the fun we miss and think we are naive and gullible. We give our time and money away. We put God and family before career and pleasure. We often go against the culture.

But Proverbs 16:25 tells us that rejecting God is the real foolishness, ending in death and destruction. The fear of the Lord is the beginning of knowledge, so those who reject God despise wisdom and instruction (Proverbs 1:7).

A godly life may seem foolish to the world, but it's the route to peace and purpose, and a godly father works to instill that understanding in his children: "Discipline your children, for in that there is hope; do not be a willing party to their death" (Proverbs 19:18 NIV).

Wise Father, Your patience is my salvation. You seek me and reveal Yourself day after day; never let me reject You! Make Yourself known to my family, and give me the patience and love to serve them in Christ.

Leaving a Lasting Legacy

A good man leaves an inheritance for his children's children,
but the sinner's wealth is laid up for the righteous.
PROVERBS 13:22 ESV

. . . .

Most people think of their legacy as the money, property, or possessions they pass on after death. That's the clear context of Proverbs 13:22. Of course we want to leave that kind of legacy and care for our wives, children, and grandchildren. It's one way we show our love for them and keep our promises—something every godly man should do.

Our legacy is much more than the material things we leave. Our legacy is spiritual, moral, and relational. It's the influence of our lives on those we love, those we know, our communities, and our world. Our true legacy is our impact in the world. Everyone leaves that kind of legacy—the good and godly person and the sinner alike. They just leave very different legacies.

So, what should we do? We should live with our legacy in mind and ask—at every decision point, at every moment of temptation, and at every opportunity to serve God and His kingdom—what we want to leave behind. Which choice will make us, our wives, children, grandchildren, and most importantly, God, proud of us? We should do that!

I praise You, O Lord, for the legacy You have left us in Christ! I thank
You for the honor of adding to Your work in this world by serving my
family and showing them all I can of You and the hope You've given us.

At the Core: Identity

Therefore, if anyone is in Christ, the new creation has come:
The old has gone, the new is here!
2 CORINTHIANS 5:17 NIV

. . . .

Who are you?

Men answer that question in many ways. We can answer it in terms of our relationships as sons, husbands, and fathers or in terms of our work or the sports we love and play. We can answer it in terms of our nationality, ethnicity, personal history, family, or generation. In fact, we are all of these and much, much more. Who we are is not one thing but the combination of many things that make each of us unique individuals.

But at the core of every man is one thing that defines how he sees himself. This fundamental identity shapes the person we become, defines all our relationships, and guides all our decisions. That core identity can come to us by virtue of our birth. Sometimes it's forced on us by society because of the color of our skin, our last name, or the circumstances we grew up in.

But the true core of our lives, the single most important thing about us, is always chosen. As Christians, we chose Christ. That fact should be the most important thing anyone knows about us. It's the choice out of which all other choices flow, that impacts everything else in life. It affects how we see ourselves, those around us, our purpose in the world, and our sense of right and wrong.

So, who are you? Is your identity in Christ the most important truth about your life?

Father of my soul, I can only find my true self in You. You've made me new in Christ and given me an eternal identity that cannot falter. Help me to serve in all my roles—husband, father, friend— with Christ as the center of all I am.

True Values

What is more, I consider everything a loss because of the surpassing worth of knowing Christ Jesus my Lord, for whose sake I have lost all things. I consider them garbage, that I may gain Christ.
PHILIPPIANS 3:8 NIV

• •

Values are those things that drive our choices.

Every day we are confronted with choices that reveal what we truly value. Is advancing our careers more valuable than time with our children? Is work more important than worship? Are our hobbies more valuable than our wives' happiness? Do we value that purchase more than staying out of debt and the financial well-being of our families? Do we value momentary pleasure more than our purpose?

In this verse, Paul expresses his greatest value. Nothing, absolutely nothing, was more valuable to him than knowing Jesus. He willingly let go of everything else and considered it little more than garbage compared to the insurmountable value of Christ in his life. Paul's core value echoed Christ's statement that loving God is the greatest commandment.

Are we like Paul, ready to value our relationship with God more than our ambition, pride, and pleasure and our desire for success, money, and status? Can we give them up? Can we serve our families based on that value rather than the world's values? Can we love them more by understanding they will always come second to the Lord? The answer to these questions has a profound impact on each man, his family, and his future.

God my Father, I want to value You above everything, but so many things distract me! Help me to focus on the eternal, and to serve my family, my friends, and this world better by never letting them compete for my devotion to You.

At the Core: Priority

*Therefore, since we are surrounded by so great a cloud of witnesses,
let us also lay aside every weight, and sin which clings so closely,
and let us run with endurance the race that is set before us,
looking to Jesus, the founder and perfecter of our faith.*
HEBREWS 12:1–2 ESV

. . . .

Living out our values means establishing priorities. Some things are important and worthy of our time, investment, and energy: an active prayer life, caring for your wife, being closely involved with your kids, striving to do better in your workplace, etc. Other things are great if we get to them. But there are things that we shouldn't do, not because they are sinful but because they distract us from what is more important.

These verses give us a way to think about our priorities. First, we should eliminate sin and everything that hinders a godly life. Things that interfere with our life in Christ or distract us from our calling should never end up on our to-do lists. Second, we should live the life God has called us to with perseverance. Staying spiritually, emotionally, relationally, and physically healthy is a priority. Fulfilling our responsibility as God's ambassadors, sons, husbands, and fathers in ways that honor God and further His kingdom isn't optional. Those responsibilities must be our priority. Finally, we should do all that while staying focused on Jesus and delighting in the joy of a life well lived.

No one disputes the wisdom found in these verses. It's just hard sometimes to understand and sometimes harder to live by. That should not keep us from trying. Achieving what's most important in life is always challenging and always worth it!

*God our Father, help us to cast off any sin that's pulling
us backward; help us to drop anything that's keeping
us from walking with You at the pace You set.*

Principles

*Trust in the LORD with all your heart and lean not on
your own understanding; in all your ways submit to him,
and he will make your paths straight.*
PROVERBS 3:5–6 NIV

• •

As fathers, we spend a great deal of time trying to get our children to trust us over their own impulses. As they grow we work to instill character and godly behavior to keep them on the "straight" path. How easy it is to understand the proverb above when we are the parent, rather than the child!

How can we live as trusting children in the challenging reality of everyday life?

First, trust God completely! The pressure we feel and the fears we face are very real. Christ's followers can and do experience very painful consequences for their faith. But we can trust God to make all things right and to reward those who serve Him.

Second, don't trust yourself! All of us have spent our lives immersed in cultures and societies that don't honor God. We learned how this world works. God's ways are so counterintuitive that our instinct is to think and act like those around us. Don't do it!

Third, submit every action and decision to God, His will, and His ways. This kind of submission isn't weak—it's incredibly strong. Submitting to God means we don't give in to the world around us or its temptations and pressures. That takes real strength and courage.

Finally, we do it God's way and walk His paths. The temptation is to wrest control over our lives from God and follow a path that makes sense to us. Adam and Eve tried that. It's never a good idea. His ways are always the best ways.

*Trustworthy Father, we have nothing to fear
from trusting You and everything to gain.*

Wisdom

Be very careful, then, how you live—not as unwise but as wise,
making the most of every opportunity, because the days are evil.
EPHESIANS 5:15–16 NIV

• •

No man wants to live with the consequences of an unwise or foolish decision. But many do. Looking back, we can't believe we were that foolish and shortsighted. But sometimes, like our own children, it's the only way to learn. In these few verses, Paul outlines guidelines for acting wisely so that we avoid the hard lessons of foolish choices.

First, recognize the reality of our times. Paul encouraged his readers to act wisely "because the days are evil." We, too, live in evil times when honoring God is disparaged as intolerant and bigoted while sinful behavior and lifestyles are celebrated. Wisdom sees our world for what it is: dangerous and destructive.

Second, be careful how you live! We can't risk acting recklessly or carelessly. Our marriages, our children, the cause of Christ, and our own futures are at stake. It's all too easy to be tempted by the pleasures of a sinful world. We may enjoy it for a time, but in the end that life destroys what we value most.

Finally, we should make the most of every opportunity. Paul's instruction is crystal clear in the context of the rest of the letter. Making the best use of time, making the most of every opportunity, rests on understanding and doing the will of God (Ephesians 5:17). The truly wise man seizes every circumstance, every choice, and every challenge as an opportunity to make the most out of doing God's will. It's the surest way to a wise and noble life.

God of wisdom, I thank You for Your constant availability. You walk with
me and offer me hope daily. Guide me to see the world for what
it is, that I may put my hope fully in You. Show me Your perspective in
my daily decisions—strengthen me to believe and to choose well.

Love! Period.

"A new command I give you: Love one another.
As I have loved you, so you must love one another."
John 13:34 NIV

. . . .

"I love God. I love being a father. I love pizza. I love the way a new car smells!" *Love*, in the English language, is a catchall word that can apply to almost any object or situation, from the deity to a pair of shoes. In the original languages of the Bible there were several words for "love," so we need to narrow our understanding when the Bible uses that word. But in these verses what Christ means is clear.

First, love isn't optional. It's a command!

Second, love is mutual. We are to love each other.

Third, the standard of our love for others is Christ's love for us. That's a tall order!

Fourth, Christian love is our surest witness. Our words don't mean much if we don't love each other.

But what does it mean to love like Christ? That isn't an easy question to answer. While there are many definitions, one practical way to think about love is "always acting in the other person's best interest." Isn't that what Christ did for us?

This kind of love isn't selfish. It's focused on the other person. It's not passive; it's active. It's not emotional; it's biblical. It doesn't cower in fear of the consequences; it's courageous.

But what is in the other person's best interest? Here are some litmus tests. When you pray, ask for godly wisdom and the leading of the Holy Spirit. What does the Bible teach? If the Bible isn't clear, ask for wise, mature Christian counsel. What would you do if that person were your own child?

Father, help us to treat everyone with the same love,
compassion, and grace we would give to our own children.

Spiritual Vitality

*And he answered, "You shall love the Lord your God with all
your heart and with all your soul and with all your strength
and with all your mind, and your neighbor as yourself."*
LUKE 10:27 ESV

• •

Every relationship, no matter how intense or important, can fade and
lose its luster.

There is no relationship more important to any man than his relationship
with God because every other relationship depends on it. When a man
loses his connection to God, his relationship with his wife, his children,
his friends, and everyone else in his life suffers.

We are called to love God with all our heart, soul, mind, and strength.
The question is how. Maintaining and developing a deeper, more vital
relationship with God requires what every other successful relationship
demands—time, intention, practice, and service.

Great relationships take time. The problem isn't God. He'll give us
all the time we want. The problem is we don't take time to pray, worship,
study His Word, and listen to His voice.

Great relationships aren't accidental. They are intentional. We have
to want spiritual vitality and intentionally do what must be done to
experience a greater degree of God's presence.

Great relationships require practice. We have to actively and
consistently do what builds up our relationship with God. Wanting it
isn't enough.

Finally, great relationships mean we serve. We invest our time,
creativity, and energy into those things that benefit the other person.
Serving brings us close to the heart of God.

If we stop working at any relationship, it grows cold. We must
intentionally and habitually invest time and energy into those practices
that bring us close to God.

O God of all relationships, strengthen us for Your work on this earth!

Character That Matters: Courage

"Have I not commanded you? Be strong and courageous.
Do not be frightened, and do not be dismayed, for the
LORD your God will be with you wherever you go."
JOSHUA 1:9 ESV

. . . .

Winston Churchill, lion of the British Empire, once famously remarked, "Courage is rightly esteemed the first of human qualities. . .because it is the quality that guarantees all the others." Our values don't matter if we don't have the courage to act on them when faced with a great challenge.

After years in Robbins Prison, Nelson Mandela said, "I learned that courage was not the absence of fear, but the triumph over it. The brave man is not he who does not feel afraid, but he who conquers that fear."

Standing on the edge of the promised land and years of war, God encouraged Joshua to "be strong and courageous" and banish fear and discouragement. But it wasn't up to Joshua to triumph over his fear. His courage rested on a solid foundation and so does ours.

We can have courage when we follow God's command. We can show our courage in the day-to-day obedience of caring for our families, working with integrity, serving in humility. If we do what He calls us to, obey His Word and honor Him, God fights for us. He will be our ally in the battle.

We can have courage because God is with us wherever our obedience takes us and in whatever battles we face. God is with us! So be strong and courageous. We have no reason to be afraid or discouraged when we are on God's side.

God of all hope, grant us, as men, the courage to stand day after
day in this world, without compromising our faith. Help us to be
resolved to speak and to act like Christ in the face of complacency
around us, opposition against us, and doubts within us.

Wholeheartedness

Whatever you do, work at it with all your heart, as working for the Lord,
not for human masters, since you know that you will receive an inheritance
from the Lord as a reward. It is the Lord Christ you are serving.
COLOSSIANS 3:23–24 NIV

• •

As fathers, we all want to help our kids find their passions in life. Sports, music, art, education—whatever they are interested in but also suited for; something that will drive them through their lives. Maybe we've found our own passion in life, or maybe we're still searching, too. But the real question is—how will our passions serve the Lord?

Sadly, many men settle "for grime when [they] could reach for glory" (Carl F. H. Henry). Their passions burn for power, possessions, pleasures, and pride. They settle for paths that give temporary pleasure but are ultimately unfulfilling and destructive.

Paul made it clear that the only passion worth living and dying for is an all-consuming passion for God. Nothing can take its place. Nothing is as satisfying or rewarding than being part of His work in the world. Most Christian men wouldn't disagree, but sometimes it's hard to see how our work and our passions align to that holy calling. We get into the weeds pursuing good things with all our might but end up empty and exhausted.

The key is knowing that as long as our passions, our interests, our work, and our efforts are done as an offering to the Lord, we are working with Him in building His kingdom. Watch your kids—they can be a lesson on this. When your daughter wants to show you a new song on the piano, or your son calls you first to let you know he just made the team—they are being an honest example of pleasing their father. We can do that with the Lord in our own works and passions. His approval is all that matters!

Father, how loving You are! We can serve
You by our passions and bring You joy in our work!

Character That Matters: Generosity

*Remember this: Whoever sows sparingly will also reap sparingly,
and whoever sows generously will also reap generously.*
2 CORINTHIANS 9:6 NIV

. . . .

Generosity is long remembered. So is stingy selfishness!

Scrooge, the main character in Dickens's *A Christmas Carol*, has become the epitome of stingy selfishness, of a man so concerned with himself he ignored the needs of all those around him, including his family, his employees, and his neighbors. But after his dramatic encounter with the ghosts of Christmas past, present, and future, he becomes so generous that "it was always said of him, that he knew how to keep Christmas well, if any man alive possessed the knowledge."

Like Scrooge, we would do well to consider generosity in light of our past, present, and future. God is generous with His children in giving us far more than we need and treating us far better than we deserve. His generosity is best expressed in His most generous gift, His own Son, Jesus. It's impossible to imagine a more generous gift to any less deserving.

Today's verse reminds us that both stingy selfishness and joyous generosity have consequences in the future—a concept that's hard enough for us, and a real challenge to communicate to our children. We need to openly practice true generosity—the kind that isn't about how much we give. (It's possible to give a great deal and not be truly generous.) Generosity is a matter of the heart attuned to a generous God. It is the result of gratitude for what He has done and trusting in what He will do.

*Generous Father, You have given us all things! You provide daily
and eternally for us as Your beloved children, and we want to
reflect that in our own lives. Open our eyes and our hearts to
opportunities to give and care for others the way You do.*

Persistence

To those who by persistence in doing good seek glory,
honor and immortality, he will give eternal life.
ROMANS 2:7 NIV

. . . .

"Nothing in the world can take the place of persistence. Talent
will not; nothing is more common than unsuccessful men with
talent. Genius will not; unrewarded genius is almost a proverb.
Education will not; the world is full of educated derelicts.
Persistence and determination alone are omnipotent. The
slogan 'Press On' has solved and always will solve the problems
of the human race."

–Calvin Coolidge, thirtieth president of
the United States of America (1872–1933)

Not everyone agrees with the "omnipotence" of persistence. In fact, all of us can think of times when we foolishly and stubbornly persisted in things that were bad for us, bad for our families, and contrary to God's will. That kind of persistence only leads to disaster. It's the kind of persistence we dread to see in our own children; how much more does God hate to see it in His children?

It's only persistence in the right direction that has the power to change our lives and the world. Paul points to persistence in four directions—in doing good, in seeking what brings glory to God, in what is honorable, and in what matters in light of eternity.

Persistence in things that don't accomplish these goals isn't persistence at all. It's just stubbornness. And stubbornness in any child invites discipline from Dad!

Loving God, I want to persist in the right things! I know I can be as
stubborn as a two-year-old when I want something that's bad for me.
Help me to grow up! Make me persistent in the things of eternity,
where the reward far outweighs anything I could attain on earth.

Humility

Be completely humble and gentle; be patient,
bearing with one another in love.
EPHESIANS 4:2 NIV

• •

On April 15, 1912, at 11:40 p.m., the British passenger liner RMS *Titanic*, on her maiden voyage, struck an iceberg in the North Atlantic and sank two hours and forty minutes later. Only 710 of 2,227 passengers and crew on board survived. Since that time, much has been made of the statement by her builders that she was "unsinkable." That arrogance and pride led her captain to take reckless and tragic risks.

It's better to live with humility than be humiliated!

Humility doesn't mean thinking less of ourselves than we should. Humility means learning and accepting the truth about ourselves. And there's no better laboratory to learn humility than your own family! Our greatest victories, greatest trials, and greatest failings will happen within this small circle.

Inside the family, humility means remembering we represent the true Father though we are unworthy; it's recognizing that each child has strengths and weaknesses as we do and acts accordingly; it's treating our wives with gentleness, showing our kids what Christ's love looks like; it's remembering our shortcomings so we are not harsh or impatient with those who struggle.

The rewards of humility are promised by God—He "gives grace to the humble" (1 Peter 5:5 NASB). As a father, and spiritual leader, what could we possibly need more than grace?

Gracious Father, teach me to hear Your warnings, to listen when
I have already made up my mind; stop me before I go sailing
ahead without You! Guard my family as I seek to be humble,
and let me always learn from them.

Honesty

Whoever gives an honest answer kisses the lips.
PROVERBS 24:26 ESV

There's an old maxim coined by Benjamin Franklin that says "Honesty is the best policy." But there are times when honesty seems like the worst possible "policy"! Our children sure seem to identify times when lying seems like the safer way to go!

From the time we learn to answer the question *"Did you do that?"* we aren't always as honest as we could or should be. We shade the truth to avoid embarrassment, save money, or stay out of trouble. Sometimes we exaggerate or downplay the truth so others will think better of us than they would if they knew the whole truth. Some men are pretty clever in the ways they are less than honest. They may not be lying, but they certainly aren't "truthing" either!

The problem with being less than honest is that the truth always and inevitably comes out. Then we are not only guilty for whatever we tried to hide, but guilty of not being honest about it. Often the dishonesty ends up hurting us more than whatever we tried to hide. We essentially get two spankings: one for the offense and one for the lie!

But beyond the consequences of being dishonest, the blessing of honesty is real intimacy with other people. Like a kiss on the lips, honesty is a sign of genuine closeness. It's refreshing to be dealt with in integrity, and the trust it builds cannot be replaced.

Father of truth, I want to be a man, a husband, a father, and a friend of integrity. Help me to put away the rationalizations that I've used to "shade" the truth. Give me the courage, and the love, to speak honestly, without concern for myself, honoring You with my words.

Learning and Growing

For this reason, since the day we heard about you, we have not stopped praying for you. We continually ask God to fill you with the knowledge of his will through all the wisdom and understanding that the Spirit gives, so that you may live a life worthy of the Lord and please him in every way: bearing fruit in every good work, growing in the knowledge of God.
COLOSSIANS 1:9–10 NIV

. . . .

Great men know there is always more to learn, and they are ready to learn it. In fact, all of us want the people we deal with—our physicians, attorneys, financial advisers, and others—to be learners. We want the best they can give us now, not what they learned years ago. We expect them to keep up!

But we all know men who aren't learners. Maybe they weren't raised to value learning. Maybe it's simply pride: they don't believe others have anything to teach them. Sometimes it's insecurity: they don't believe they can master new things. But most of the time, it's just neglect and laziness. We're comfortable without the hard work of learning, so why put out the effort? We see it in our kids all during their school years, but we don't always recognize it in ourselves.

People can get away with not learning in some things but never in their spiritual lives. Today's verses make it clear that "a life worthy of the Lord" is a life that is growing in the knowledge of God through the wisdom and understanding of the Spirit. The truth is that no matter how much we know of God and His wisdom there is always more to know.

Have you learned something new about God this week, this month, or this year? What's your plan for tomorrow, next week, next year?

Father, You alone are the source of all knowledge.
Make us teachable! Help our minds and hearts to become
hungry again and our eyes to see You in all that we learn.

Commitments That Matter

Now all has been heard; here is the conclusion of the matter: Fear God and keep his commandments, for this is the duty of all mankind.
ECCLESIASTES 12:13 NIV

• •

We all make commitments. And we all know some commitments matter more than others. If we can't keep our commitment to have coffee with a friend, it's not a big deal. If we don't keep our commitments to our wives and children, it's a very big deal! (They're tracking it!)

What we are committed to shapes and makes up much of our lives. There are some things to which we must make unwavering, permanent commitments if we expect to leave a legacy that matters.

The first and most fundamental commitment any Christian man must make is his commitment to God and the Christian life. It has to be a non-negotiable. No matter what comes, no matter what challenges we face, no matter how great our successes or failures, our commitment to God is the star we steer by and the compass that guides our days.

There are plenty of examples of men who have given up on their commitment to God and following Him. All of them have some things in common. First, in a moment of trial and temptation they wavered and broke their commitment. Second, their grip on God gradually loosened. Finally, in the end they and those they loved suffered, and they left a woeful legacy.

How committed to God are you today? Are you wavering? Are you losing your grip? Have you become forgetful that the Father's commitment to you is the reason you can be committed to Him at all?

Unwavering Father, how we thank You for Your commitment to us! You are the anchor of our relationship, not us. But we want to be good sons! Help us to love You more and to walk with You, committed to You through the power of the Holy Spirit.

Honoring Family

But if a widow has children or grandchildren, these should learn first of all to put their religion into practice by caring for their own family and so repaying their parents and grandparents, for this is pleasing to God.
1 TIMOTHY 5:4 NIV

. . . .

Next to a man's commitment to God, there is no commitment more important than his commitment to be a godly son, brother, husband, and father. Nothing will leave a more lasting impact on the generations to come, and nothing will matter more to him in the end.

Sadly, it seems that many men have abandoned their critical role in the family to pursue their own wants, needs, and desires. They seem to care little for the impact of their choices on their wives, their children, and future generations. Being a godly husband and father just doesn't seem important. Nothing could be further from the truth!

We are called to lead our families in faithfully following God, to willingly sacrifice, to love our spouses like Christ loved the Church, and to guide our children to a life devoted to God and His service. We are called to be protectors, providers, and examples of godly living.

It's true: There is no such thing as a perfect man, husband, or father. We all make mistakes, have regrets, and wish we had done some things differently. But perfection isn't required. A commitment to live for God and lead and love our family is.

God, You are the perfect Father and Provider. Give me the strength to serve my family, and when I fail, give me the grace to admit it and to begin again. Daily, show me how to be a faithful man to the most important people in my life.

God's People

*Do nothing out of selfish ambition or vain conceit. Rather,
in humility value others above yourselves, not looking to your
own interests but each of you to the interests of the others.*
PHILIPPIANS 2:3–4 NIV

• •

"To live above with the saints we love, oh that will be glory! To live below
with the saints we know, that's another story!"

To leave a godly legacy we must not only be committed to God and
our families, but to the people of God, His Church. That's not always
easy. Sometimes conflict troubles the church. It's easy to be disappointed
or discouraged. But that doesn't mean we should walk away from God's
people. We need each other. And even if we as individuals don't feel
that need, our families need the connection and encouragement of a
local body of believers.

Today's verse challenges us in several ways. First, we are not to act
out of selfish ambition or vain conceit. All too often our disappointment
comes from bruised egos and taking offense. Our commitment to the
Church must go beyond our wants and needs and rest on a deep loyalty
to the family of God.

Second, we are to value others. Even those who hurt and disappoint
us are valuable and worthy of our grace and forgiveness. We, too, need
grace, forgiveness, and loyalty when we fail and disappoint others.

Finally, we should care about and do what is good for others. It's
God's Church and they are God's people. Perhaps the most powerful
question we can ask is, "What can I do for you?" We are all guilty of
asking, "What can the Church do for me?"

*Heavenly Father, You called us into this fellowship; You gave
Your Son to create it—don't let our love for Jesus be so small
that we neglect our brothers and sisters in the Lord!*

God's Work in the World

*"Go therefore and make disciples of all nations, baptizing them
in the name of the Father and of the Son and of the Holy Spirit,
teaching them to observe all that I have commanded you."*
MATTHEW 28:19–20 ESV

. . . .

God is at work in the world! Many doubt it or ignore it, but it's still true.
Also, God will accomplish His plans and purposes. . .with or without us!

The only real issue is whether or not we will be part of what God is
doing. In the end, the most exciting life is one fully devoted to the greatest
cause. Nothing can match the grandeur, significance, or value of being
on a mission with God.

Sadly, there are many myths and misunderstandings. Serving God
isn't a profession. It's a lifestyle. Serving God doesn't mean giving up
everything we enjoy. God isn't a killjoy! Nor does it mean leaving the life
we have and going to some faraway place. We can serve God right where
we are. In fact, if you're a dad, your first disciples are right under your
own roof. It's doubtful you will ever have a chance to influence anyone
toward the Lord more than your own kids. A man's day is crowded with
responsibilities and obligations, and many think they don't have time. But
we all know we make time for what is most important to us.

Every man is gifted and called to serve God, and each of us is uniquely
equipped and positioned to make a difference in the world right where
we are. . .if we'll do it.

That's the real question, isn't it? Will we?

*Holy God, thank You for the privilege of shaping and influencing
our kids for Christ! Help us to teach and to guide our first disciples
into a deep and sustaining relationship with You. And open our
eyes to those around us whom we can help grow in Christ.*

The Power of Presence

"And surely I am with you always, to the very end of the age."
MATTHEW 28:20 NIV

• •

It's one of the most comforting promises in the entire Bible. Jesus is God Emmanuel, God with us who never leaves or forsakes us.

Presence matters. Being with those we love matters to our wives, children, and friends. Sometimes just being there, just being with those we love, is the very best thing we can do. But being there for those we love only happens if we make it a priority. But it's not always easy.

There are times when being away from family isn't a man's choice. Work and other obligations can demand long absences or that we miss important moments. That's not the point. Our wives and children understand that.

Here are some suggestions. First, make your presence a priority. Family events go on your calendar first! Build the rest of your life around them. Second, find a way to be with your wife and kids every day. Give them your time no matter how tired or stressed you are. When you are with them, be *with* them. Leave the briefcase, the hassles, and the worries at work and focus on them. When you can't be there, find a way to be there. Skype, telephone, e-mail, write notes and cards, Facebook message or Twitter, send flowers or gifts. Do something that shows your thoughts and your heart are with them. You'll never regret it.

Finally, make sure that when your kids and grandchildren leaf through the family photo albums, they'll find pictures of you! By God's design you are a powerful influence.

> God, You have not only made Yourself known to us, You have made Your presence felt by actually living in us! The power of having You with us through everything gives us hope. Help us to give that same hope to those You've entrusted to us.

The Future

I consider that our present sufferings are not worth comparing with the glory that will be revealed in us.
ROMANS 8:18 NIV

• •

Some men live in the past. Others live only in the present. But if becoming a father doesn't make you think about the future, nothing will!

The future is life's great, undiscovered territory. We know the past. At least we think we do. We can see the present, at least most of it. But no one accurately and truly knows the future. All we can do is make our best guess. There are too many unknown factors that are completely out of our control for us to predict the future. We just wish we could, especially when we have a family looking to us for leadership.

But this is a world of cause and effect, of action and reaction. What we choose today always and inevitably matters in the future. Sometimes what we think is a trivial decision has the greatest impact. And we know that God has revealed great truths and magnificent wisdom. So how do we live with an eye on the future?

First, don't let the past determine the future. Whatever happened in the past need not control our present decisions or future lives. Second, act ethically, not expediently. Make wise long-term decisions, not easy short-term choices. Third, trust God, His will and His ways, not what you see around you. Remember, God, not our present circumstances, controls the future.

Finally, ask yourself, "Do I want this choice to be part of the story of my life I tell my children or grandchildren?"

God of the past, present, and future, You alone know the beginning from the end. And You have called us Your children. Your great promise will sustain us—that You have a plan for us, to give us hope and a future.

Live above the Line

But you, man of God, flee from all this, and pursue righteousness, godliness, faith, love, endurance and gentleness. Fight the good fight of the faith. Take hold of the eternal life to which you were called when you made your good confession in the presence of many witnesses.
1 TIMOTHY 6:11–12 NIV

• •

In 1990, the one-of-a-kind Hubble Space Telescope was launched from the space shuttle *Discovery*. Not long after, it was discovered that the images coming from the Hubble were blurred and out of focus. This massive piece of equipment was designed to do one thing, and in fact it needed corrective lenses!

When it comes to living the Christian life, it's easy for things to get out of focus, out of sync with our design. Sometimes it's hard to see the line that separates godly conduct from culturally acceptable conduct. We need the corrective lens of the Holy Spirit to help us see clearly and live life above the line.

Living above the line is sometimes as simple as a matter of what we *flee*. To begin, 1 Timothy 6:1–10 contains a long list of things the man of God should run away from. Second, Paul tells Timothy to pursue righteousness, godliness, faith, love, endurance, and gentleness. Finally, Paul reminded Timothy, as his spiritual son, that living above the line is a fight, but it's a good fight.

Men who leave a great and godly heritage for their children see clearly what must be left behind and what must be sought and are willing to pay the price. They don't live below the line, below the minimum standard. They don't live at the line, just barely scraping by. They strive to live above the line!

Gracious God, our Father, help us to be men, husbands, fathers of courage and to flee those things that would drag us away from You. Grant us peace through obedience.

Listening

"Now then, my children, listen to me; blessed are those who keep my ways. Listen to my instruction and be wise; do not disregard it."
PROVERBS 8:32–33 NIV

• •

Listening is always harder than talking, as any father knows. It seems like kids are wired to ignore what we say, while they can go on endlessly about something they want to talk about. But it's part of the deal—we all want others to know how we feel, to understand why we act and see things as we do. When people don't listen to us, we feel insignificant and disrespected.

It's easy to forget other people need the same thing from us. When we don't listen to our wives, children, friends, and coworkers, they feel ignored, uncared for, and mistreated. But when we listen well, we open the door to greater intimacy and understanding; we build trust and strengthen the bonds of our relationships. That's why listening is so important.

Before anyone else, we need to listen to God and His Spirit in our lives. All too often when we pray we talk too much and listen too little. Our families come next. We need to listen to our wives. How else can we know their hopes, dreams, and fears? We need to listen to our children. It's the best way to earn our place in their lives for the rest of our lives. Our wives don't always need to know what we think. Our children don't always need correction or a lecture. Sometimes they just need us to love them enough to let them talk, listen carefully, empathize with their feelings, and show them the dignity and respect every person longs for.

Isn't that what God does for us when we pray?

Father, You are the model Listener! You are always available and always interested in us. In fact, there's no way to exhaust You when we pray— You could listen for hours! Help us to become like You toward our families and those around us. Above all, help us to listen when You speak!

Laugh!

*Our mouths were filled with laughter, our tongues
with songs of joy. Then it was said among the nations,
"The LORD has done great things for them."*
PSALM 126:2 NIV

• •

Oh, lighten up!

Life is serious business. But that doesn't mean we can't find joy and laughter in each day if we look for it. All too often men who feel the weight of their responsibilities wear that burden on their faces. Here's the question: Why would our children follow us into the Christian life if we were constantly joyless and unhappy? No one wants that kind of life.

Enjoying life is largely a matter of perspective. For us, a snowy day may mean shoveling the driveway, a slow commute to work, and the frustration of other drivers on slippery streets. To our children, a snowy day is filled with the boundless potential for fun. There's no school! The snow is beautiful. Sledding is great fun, and there's nothing better than pelting your sister with snowballs. It's all a matter of perspective.

We need to learn how to rejoice in the great things God has done and is doing even in the hard times. Let's learn to laugh at ourselves. We all do some amazingly funny things—we don't mean to, but we do! Learn to laugh with others and enjoy being with them. Smile at the silly but annoying things other people do every day. Throw yourself into life and enjoy the trip!

So, lighten up! Have some fun. The Lord has done great things!

*Good Father, You've given us reason beyond measure to rejoice!
You have given us abundant life in Your Son, Jesus, but we let
ourselves fall into fear and worry. You will always be with us
and in every circumstance give us the power of joy!*

Apologize

Godly sorrow brings repentance that leads to salvation.
2 CORINTHIANS 7:10 NIV

• •

In *Love Story*, the famous book and 1970 movie, a dying young woman looks at her lover and says, "Love means never having to say you're sorry." Nothing could be further from the truth! There is little that damages relationships more than the prideful refusal to admit we were wrong, take responsibility for our actions, and apologize to those we injured. It's a basic character lesson we try to instill in our children from their earliest years. Why? Because refusing to apologize when you're wrong will compound over time into arrogance and pride.

At the core of our faith is the notion of repentance. In a very real sense, when we confess our sins and repent, we apologize to God for the harm we've done to Him and others. That act opens the door to His grace, forgiveness, and new beginnings. All who choose the path of repentance are welcomed. Those who refuse to repent lock themselves away from God's love and care.

Apologizing is also essential for our health. In Celebrate Recovery's Eight Recovery Principles, an eight-step guide for getting over addictions, we read:

Principle 4: Openly examine and confess my faults to God, to myself, and to someone I trust.

Principle 6: Evaluate all my relationships; offer forgiveness to those who have hurt me and make amends for the harm I've done to others. . .

Finally, when we apologize, we set a standard and an example others can follow to heal broken relationships and grow in grace and humility.

*Father, help me to be quick to admit to others when
I've wronged them and to apologize with real humility.*

Conduct That Matters: Work Hard

And then I will be able to boast on the day
of Christ that I did not run or labor in vain.
PHILIPPIANS 2:16 NIV

• •

There is little to admire in a lazy man. No employer wants to hire one. No woman wants to be married to one, and no child is proud of a lazy father.

We shouldn't be surprised. When God created Adam, He "put him in the garden of Eden to work it and keep it" (Genesis 2:15 ESV). Before God created Eve and gave Adam the responsibilities of a husband and father, God gave him work to do. Work isn't the result of the fall. It just got harder after the fall (Genesis 3:17–19).

Work isn't part of the curse but was meant as an expression of our nature as beings created in the image of God and in partnership with God's creative work in the world. Successfully completing a task and doing a good job brings a sense of satisfaction and self-esteem to a man that little else can bring. No wonder work is so important to us!

In his admonition to the Philippians, Paul pointed out that his work wasn't in vain and he could boast in the day of Christ. Paul put in the effort and worked hard at what mattered most. Paul did his work so well that he could boast not only in his accomplishment, but also in the way he worked. So should we.

Holy Father, You have given us the blessing of work so that we can
enjoy providing for our families and for those in need the way You do.
We get to join You in the blessing of giving! Help us to put all
our heart into what we do so that You will be honored.

Build Others Up

You then, my son, be strong in the grace that is in Christ Jesus.
And the things you have heard me say in the presence of many
witnesses entrust to reliable people who will also be qualified to teach
others. Join with me in suffering, like a good soldier of Christ Jesus.
2 TIMOTHY 2:1–3 NIV

• •

There are plenty of people who are ready to tell our children, our wives, our friends, and our coworkers what's wrong with them. They don't need to hear it from us!

What they need to hear is what's right with them—why we are proud of them, why we love them, and why they are a gift to us and the world. Sure, we need to offer some correction now and then, but it should be small in proportion to the encouragement we offer. There aren't many people in their lives who will do that for them, but we can.

Paul's adopted son, Timothy, was an outstanding young man who faced unfair criticism. There were plenty of people ready to tell Timothy what was wrong with him. But Paul's place in his life was entirely different. Paul taught Timothy who Jesus was and who Timothy was in Jesus.

First, Paul encouraged Timothy. "Be strong in the grace that is in Christ Jesus."

Second, this letter was part of Paul's long-standing support, instruction, and help. These were things Timothy had heard before.

Third, Paul's praise for Timothy and his teachings were public. He said these things "in the presence of many witnesses."

Fourth, Timothy was responsible to do the same for others.

Finally, Paul invited Timothy to join him as he followed Christ.

It's an example worth following.

God of all encouragement, You've redeemed us for Your own good
pleasure! You sing over us! We praise You with all we are!

Conduct That Matters: Sacrifice

Therefore, I urge you, brothers and sisters, in view of
God's mercy, to offer your bodies as a living sacrifice,
holy and pleasing to God—this is your true and proper worship.
ROMANS 12:1 NIV

• •

We don't use the word *sacrifice* much, except in baseball and for those who serve in the military. Maybe that's because so few of us ever really sacrifice.

Sacrifice means surrendering something precious for the good of another. Sacrifice is always costly, painful, and challenging. But we should remember that the foundation of our faith is Christ's sacrifice for us. He surrendered heaven to suffer and die as a sacrifice for our sins.

A sacrificial life pleases God. It is true and proper worship. But that sacrifice is taken up "in view of God's mercy." Christ's sacrifice proved His love for us. It changed the world and it changed the future. It brought hope and healing, grace and goodness, joy and peace. So we follow His example.

There is no more powerful demonstration of love and courage than when a man willingly sacrifices his wants and desires for his wife, his children, and the cause of Christ. Sacrifice, not selfishness, is the stuff of heroes. Such loving sacrifice sends a powerful message and leaves a lasting legacy well worth whatever it cost.

Generous Father, You gave us Your own Son as a sacrifice for our sins.
How can we even consider what we give up as a sacrifice? We can only offer
You back what You've given us! Even so, help us to understand where and
how we can give up our own desires and needs to serve others.

A Coach's World

*You have heard me teach things that have been confirmed
by many reliable witnesses. Now teach these truths to other
trustworthy people who will be able to pass them on to others.*
2 TIMOTHY 2:2 NLT

. . . .

Coaching has become commonplace from little league to corporate America. Many companies have discovered that coaching or mentoring is the best way to groom their people to advance, take charge, and take risks. Employers don't want you to stop learning new skills.

You may be getting some of your own coaching from church. You may not think of church as coaching, but it can be. It should be. Barnabas coached Paul. Paul coached Timothy. Timothy coached his own congregation. Great coaching makes great teams.

As Christian men we start with learning biblical basics, but we never learn it all. Our entire lives can be spent being coached *and* coaching others.

All fathers need to *become* godly coaches. People, starting with our own kids, need authentic mentors. The world is full of the other kind. Jesus never had much good to say about those spiritual pretenders. Matthew 23:27 (MSG) says, " 'You're hopeless, you religion scholars and Pharisees! Frauds! You're like manicured grave plots, grass clipped and the flowers bright, but six feet down it's all rotting bones and worm-eaten flesh.' "

When we think we've learned all there is to learn, we need to think again. God never wants us to stop learning, stop sharing, or stop growing, and He wants us to pass that blessing on.

Find a coach. Be a coach. Encourage a coach. There's a lot of growing just waiting on your response.

Patient Father, we praise You for Your commitment to make us like Your Son. Help us to bring our children along following Your example.

Superhero Substitute

*And we have seen and testify that the Father
has sent the Son as Savior of the world.*
1 JOHN 4:14 NKJV

• •

More than 125,000 people attend Comic-Con each year. This annual convention is dedicated to comic books and everything developed from those stories. Each month, more than $250,000,000 is spent on the most popular comic books. Worldwide ticket sales for movies that are based on comic books are in the billions. At least three collectible comic books have sold for more than a million dollars each. Comic book heroes are big business.

Maybe you've been to see a superhero movie. Maybe you have your own collection of comic books. Maybe you even geek out about the backstory of a hero's world.

People love superheroes because they're passionate about identifying with someone with the power to rescue people from bad situations.

First Timothy 1:15 (MSG) says, "Here's a word you can take to heart and depend on: Jesus Christ came into the world to save sinners."

We're born. We sin. We need rescue.

Jesus isn't make-believe. He is more than a compelling story. He's God's champion. He faced the toughest enemy mankind has ever known—and won.

We read comic books because we want a hero. We want to be rescued. We want everything to be all right in the world. It's a need that humanity has and that comic book writers have always known. Maybe someone you know who's into comic books might like to hear about the reality behind those colorful pages. Maybe it's a good way to introduce your kids to the Savior who comes to our rescue!

*Jesus, our Rescuer and Savior! Your story is bolder and more colorful
than any comic book or superhero movie—You came in weakness
but rose in power; You came in disguise but revealed Yourself to
those who loved You; You will return to rescue us for all time!*

The House That Fifty-Seven Cents Bought

Honor God with everything you own; give him the first and the best.
PROVERBS 3:9 MSG

• •

The year was 1912. The Reverend Russell Conwell led the congregation of Grace Baptist Church in Philadelphia. He struggled with the lack of space for Sunday school classes.

Unknown to the reverend, there was a little girl named Hattie May Wiatt that also saw the problem. She began to save pennies, nickels, and dimes. Each coin meant something she had denied herself. She became sick and died before a new church could be built.

Hattie's mother told Reverend Conwell about her daughter's savings. The handful of coins seemed small and insignificant when compared to the need, but it seems Hattie's big idea was much bigger than she realized. The coins were all converted to pennies, and the church sold Hattie's *pennies* for nearly $250.

Hattie's example inspired the Wiatt Mite Society. They used the $250 to purchase a nearby house for church use. The first classes of Temple College were held in the house that fifty-seven cents bought.

Our dreams are only the right size if they're bigger than we can manage on our own. If God gets no credit because we do everything ourselves, then all we've done is fulfill a self-achieving dream. God always dreams bigger than we do, shows up when we have nowhere to turn, and makes the impossible possible.

God wants us to be generous. Hattie May Wiatt's story shows that even a small gift can help achieve a God-sized dream that brings honor, the One who loved us enough to give us—everything.

O Father, how much You multiply our smallest efforts when they are done in faith! Jesus fed thousands from the small donation of a little boy. You build Your kingdom on the small and seemingly insignificant things to demonstrate that You alone are God.

Intentional Investing

Parents rejoice when their children turn out well;
wise children become proud parents.
PROVERBS 23:24 MSG

• •

We all carry a few labels: man, boss, employee, husband, dad, or coach. Many of the labels we wear involve teaching.

If you're a dad, homework never ends, although some may refuse to accept their assignments.

Being a dad is hard work. Your children look to you as a model. Your behavior can become their behavior. What you accept is what they accept. What you say is. . .well, you get the idea.

When you're at home, work at being intentional as a parent. When you ask your children to do, be, or say something different than what they see in your life, they can be confused. They may think, *But that's not what Dad does!*

Intentional dads understand their legacy comes at a price; they are long-term investors. And the coin of investing is time: time with them, time in prayer, time to listen, time to set the right examples. But it can return a thousand percent, not just in your children, but also in your grandchildren.

It's never too late to ask God to be intentional about helping you help your children. They need you, you love them, and God supplies the action plan. Find what you need in His Word.

The good news is you don't have to be perfect to be intentional. Admit mistakes, ask your children for forgiveness, and then return to the plan.

Father, You, more than any other, are an intentional dad!
You have a plan for each of Your children and the will to see
it done. Help us to submit to You and live Your plan, and to
do the same with the children You've entrusted to us.

Within the Boundaries

Keep your minds on whatever is true, pure, right, holy,
friendly, and proper. Don't ever stop thinking about
what is truly worthwhile and worthy of praise.
PHILIPPIANS 4:8 CEV

• •

Gaze at ranch land and you'll find fences. Ranchers will often say they get along better with their neighbors when there's a good fence between their properties. Why? The property lines are defined by boundaries. Children learn this early on. Listening without interruption, respecting closed doors, not taking things without asking permission. Growing up is all about learning boundaries.

In our own lives, we have the boundaries of truth, purity, righteousness, holiness, friendliness, and propriety.

Breaking down those boundaries will always make purity less pure, truth less true, and holiness less holy. Broken boundaries allow us to accept bad behavior, participate in poor decision-making, and treat others with less respect.

God wants us to embrace holy boundaries and teach them to our children. We can use boundaries to keep other people out, but maybe God wants us to use boundaries to keep His ideas *in*. We can be content within the fence when we realize it's for our good, a part of God's plan, and that it reminds us we were born with a purpose.

Why would God want to protect us with boundaries if there was no plan for our good?

Enjoy and model the freedom to improve, grow, and develop the life within the boundaries.

Heavenly Father, how we often push the boundaries You've set
to bring us peace and life! How often we see it in our own kids
but miss it in our own lives. Help us to embrace Your purpose.

An Imperfect Parent

*Watch out that no poisonous root of bitterness
grows up to trouble you, corrupting many.*
HEBREWS 12:15 NLT

. . . .

Life can be unfair.

She hadn't been perfect. She made her son choose between his father and herself. The boy was twelve and wanted to spend time with his dad. That decision meant his mother would have almost nothing to do with him for more than thirty years.

As a man, that boy wondered what he had done that was so wrong.

In her sixties, his mom underwent a life-threatening operation. The son showed up and both were changed. The son determined to forgive even though she had never asked. He determined to love even when she resisted. He rejected bitterness even though there were plenty of memories to inspire it.

In time, the mother said four words that were long overdue, "I love you, son." These were sweet words. She told him stories of his childhood that he didn't remember. He caught a glimpse of the mother she wanted to be, but hadn't.

Not every parent gets it right, and it doesn't take such extreme circumstances to frustrate a child's life. Let us, as fathers, be on guard and remember the admonition of Colossians 3:21 (NIV), "Fathers, do not embitter your children, or they will become discouraged." Avoiding a root of bitterness is far better than having to uproot it later.

*O God of peace, help us to bring peace to our families
and give no cause for bitterness in our children. Guard them
against any seed we may plant that might grow in them and bring
them trouble. Humble us, Lord, and give us wisdom to serve You well.*

An Unusual Canvas

• •

Paul Smith was born in the 1920s. While other children attended school he lived with cerebral palsy. He couldn't attend school or even dress himself. It affected speech and physical ability. However, inside a body with limited muscle control was an artist.

In the mid-1930s, Paul discovered a typewriter in the neighbor's trash. He rescued the machine and began to create art. The meticulous repositioning of the paper and specific keystrokes allowed Paul to create typewriter art that looked very much like traditional charcoal drawings.

Hour after hour Paul would use his more stable hand to steady the other and work at striking a key. Paul would reposition the paper and start over. He had just accomplished one keystroke in the thousands that would create beauty.

Friend Jim Mitch said, "[Paul] developed a distinct, beautiful way of creating art. . . Paul's technique required that the entire picture must be planned before he started."

Paul passed away in 2007, but his is the story of a marathon. While he could never run physically, he did have a passion to remain steady, determined, and composed. His art needed to be shared. Once he found the typewriter, this man who struggled to speak created masterpieces from his room in an Oregon nursing home.

God has given each of our kids something unique. It may be obvious, or like Paul Smith, it may be hidden so deep that no one would guess it's even there. As dads, our job is to know our children, help them collect life experiences, and reach beyond the surface to bring out the treasure buried inside.

You, O Lord, have buried treasure in each one of us. Give us the perseverance to dig and to find what You've placed there, not only in ourselves, but in our families. Show us how to use every experience, good or bad, to glorify You on the earth.

Consumer Testing

It is absolutely clear that God has called you to a free life. Just make sure that you don't use this freedom as an excuse to do whatever you want to do and destroy your freedom. Rather, use your freedom to serve one another in love; that's how freedom grows. For everything we know about God's Word is summed up in a single sentence: Love others as you love yourself. That's an act of true freedom.
GALATIANS 5:13–14 MSG

• •

One hundred–item buffets. Have it the way you want. All you can eat. Refills are free. Don't leave hungry.

We are given anything we might possibly want as long as we pay the price. We consume food, clothes, automobiles, news, sports, and amusements of all kinds. Marketers are quick to reach out to consumers, and especially young people with more time and discretionary income.

There is a love affair with choice, and, being spoiled by it, we're frustrated and sometimes angry if the selection doesn't meet our standards.

What does God's Word say? "Keep your lives free from the love of money and be content with what you have, because God has said, 'Never will I leave you; never will I forsake you.'" (Hebrews 13:5 NIV).

God isn't so much anti-stuff as He is pro-contentment. Contentment may best be described as being satisfied in God's presence, thankful for His gifts, and believing God knows what we really need.

Godly contentment desires to be consumed with His goodness and is useful in showing others His love.

Father, You created all things, and did so for our enjoyment. But we have taken these things out of context—thinking to make our lives fuller, we have become poorer. Forgive us for such a childish mistake! Help us to be content in You and with what You provide.

Panic without Proof

Blessed are you who run to him.
PSALM 34:8 MSG

• •

In the fall of 2014, America was overwhelmed. News had been released that the entire country was to be inundated with unprecedented snow depths that would cripple the nation, and only seasoned or quick-thinking survivalists would make it to spring.

The news caused fear. The news was shared hundreds of thousands of times on social media. The news became news.

Reputable news sources began to share the information with their news consumers, but within a news cycle or two, the truth was revealed. American citizens felt duped.

The website that originated the story has a tab that reads "About Us." One click of that tab and visitors read, "[We are a] satirical and entertainment website. We only use invented names in all our stories."

Believable, plausible, and *terrifying* were all words used in connection with the story, but the real intent of the piece was not to inform but entertain. Few checked. Many panicked.

God has always wanted us to test our sources. First John 4:1 (MSG) says, "Don't believe everything you hear. Carefully weigh and examine what people tell you. Not everyone who talks about God comes from God."

How do we weigh and examine what we hear and read about God? Through His Word, the Bible.

People may not have an "About Us" tab for us to check, but the ideas they present are either confirmed or denied by what God has already told us. God's Word is always enough.

Father, thank You for making Yourself known in truth and love.

A Community on the Corner

God is love. Whoever lives in love lives in God, and God in them.
1 JOHN 4:16 NIV

• •

The barbershop sits at the end of the block. The chairs and decor were installed in 1961, a few years prior to a man landing on the moon. Until recently, the founder of the shop was the first to greet guests. His name was in neon, just to the right of the rotating barber pole.

Inside you'll find men who've made this a regular stop for decades, men who raised their sons to come there. One conversation with the owner made it clear why they returned.

He was a great barber, but he understood most people just want to be heard. His gentle questions highlighted an unexpected compassion. He remembered what you told him. If a farmer mentioned a struggle, the barber followed up the next visit to see if things had improved.

That barber demonstrated what most men look for in friendship. We want friends who are dependable, listen, remember when they need to, and forget when they don't.

Jesus offered that example, but He wants that example to shine through us.

It's easy to get trapped in our own trouble, but other people may need us, and we need them.

That barbershop was a community. It was a place where haircuts were secondary to understanding. It was a throwback to a simpler time and an example of the best of human compassion. Most miss this barber for reasons that have nothing to do with hair.

We don't need to cut hair to learn this barber's skill. Perhaps he learned from someone far more compassionate.

Holy God, Your own Son called His disciples "friends"
because He was able to share His heart and soul with them.
Help me to be that kind of friend to someone.

The Best Ingredients

"Announce the Message of God's good news to one and all."
MARK 16:15 MSG

• •

Who knew you could take dough, some tomato sauce, cheese, and a few favorite ingredients, toss them in the oven and create a masterpiece? It seems too easy. It tastes too good. It's the fuel of kids all over the world!

The history of pizza is a little cloudy. It could have come from Egypt, Greece, or Italy. Each country can argue the point. In America, our link to pizza comes directly from Italy, and the first place it was sold was New York, although Connecticut argues the point.

Statistics show there is more than 250 pounds of pepperoni used in making pizzas each year. Pizzerias average 55 pizza boxes used each day. Ninety-four percent of us eat pizza regularly. Around the world, five billion pizzas are sold each year. And to show the wild popularity of the "pie," there is a pizzeria in Alaska with annual sales of more than six million dollars!

Why is pizza so popular? It's the combination of ingredients that makes it magical. In the same way, God has given us some impressive ingredients to deliver a message people crave. They include "love, joy, peace, patience, kindness, goodness, faithfulness, gentleness, and self-control" (Galatians 5:22–23 NLT). Taken all together, they are an effective and tasty combination!

God wants our lives to have flavor, because the world around us is hungry. When we share the good news we've been given, we can develop a greater craving in those who hear it, or it can leave an aftertaste that is memorable for all the wrong reasons. Build a message on the ingredients God values, real and tasty!

God of heaven and earth, how delicious are all Your ways!

Leave the Museum Rejoicing

Jesus Christ is the same yesterday, today, and forever.
HEBREWS 13:8 NLT

· ·

We all take our kids to a museum to teach them our history. The exhibits depict the best and worst of our past. We can be encouraged, entertained, or thoughtful when we leave a museum. The finest examples of museums engage our memories.

Museums share the narrative of a story that is either cautionary or makes us long for the simplicity we once knew or now long for.

We wouldn't want to *live* in a museum because it only represents something that once was. We *visit* because we want knowledge or entertainment. We leave because there is real life existing in the here and now.

The Bible is filled with history keepers who explain what God had done for the people who followed Him. Their role was important and served a great purpose.

When the people remembered a faithful God, they always found a reason to praise Him.

If we look back at our own past, we'll discover that even when we made bad choices, God was faithful to love and forgive. We shouldn't be surprised when gratitude to God is the result of remembering.

While the faithfulness of God doesn't change, neither do His commands. Nor does His willingness to guide, love, forgive, and provide.

God doesn't want His people to only live in His Faithfulness Museum because as wonderful as that is, His faithfulness reaches into real life for real people right now.

Let God redeem your past by walking with Him today.

*Eternal Father, You alone can redeem our
own personal history and give us a real future.*

God's Spending Limit?

"For all the animals of the forest are mine,
and I own the cattle on a thousand hills."
PSALM 50:10 NLT

• •

Accountants are valuable when it comes to keeping track of expenses. They know what assets have value and which have become liabilities. Budgets are an accountant's playground, and they're really good at making sure all expenses and payments are noted.

God's economy is a bit different. God cares less about numbers and more about people.

If God owns everything, then He can use anything to do the most amazing things. God doesn't even get upset at the cost it takes to rescue people. He just keeps relentlessly pursuing with incredible compassion.

He's a lavish God who makes sunsets, forests, stars, and oceans for us to enjoy.

If God did have an accountant, they would probably say, "Why spend another dime? There's a lot of people down there that will never thank You. I'm not sure if You're aware of it or not, but that sunset last night exceeded the budget!"

God created everything. He needs nothing. However, He wants each of us to know Him, and He'll keep seeking until He finds us, rescues us, and makes plans for us to live with Him forever. He's a relentless Father who lavishes His children with blessings—though we don't always thank Him properly. A feeling every father can relate to!

God never has to worry about running out of resources. In fact, He never worries at all. He just keeps loving real people with real compassion leading to real change. And when He asks you to share what you have, it's all about experiencing a similar sense of joy that He felt when He gave His all for you.

Generous Father, I pause now to give You thanks
for all that You do for me as my true Father!

Here to Represent

GOD hates cheating in the marketplace;
he loves it when business is aboveboard.
PROVERBS 11:1 MSG

• •

Today, if we want to weigh something, we usually put it on an electronic scale and get a digital readout providing the result. There's a more ancient method that's still in use. This method allows someone to put a weight on half of a two-sided scale. On the second half, they would place what they were either buying or selling. When the scale was balanced, there was an equal amount on both sides. That's how people used to figure a price when buying or selling.

Sometimes business owners altered the weights. If they were selling something, they wanted the weight to weigh less so they didn't have to give as much to the buyer. If they were buying something, they would use a heavier weight so they could get more from the seller.

God calls this cheating and so would a customer. God would be displeased and so would the person who discovered the fraud. God could forgive, but a customer might never forget. (Try giving a bigger piece of cake to one child than another and see what kind of reaction you get!)

As Christians, we're asked to bring integrity with us to the workplace. God wants us to represent Him in the way we do business. We should be willing to go further than we have to in order to make things right.

We're God's ambassadors. We're not selective servants. We're not undercover believers. We're God's representatives to people who are all too familiar with dishonesty. Our story of God's faithfulness will always bear a hint of tarnish when we can't remember where we left our integrity.

*Father, You are true and just, always saying what
You mean. Help us to remember that our words
and actions reflect on You, our God and Savior.*

The Blessing Conspiracy

*As God's chosen people, holy and dearly loved, clothe yourselves
with compassion, kindness, humility, gentleness and patience.*
COLOSSIANS 3:12 NIV

• •

George is a secret agent. Those he serves don't know his name and rarely
know what he looks like, but they remember what he *does*.

George visits a lot of restaurants. Usually he orders a cup of coffee.
He's on a fact-finding mission. He quietly pays attention to what's going
on around him. He puts one or two tables on his short list and asks the
wait staff for help in his *blessing conspiracy*.

George travels a lot. He doesn't know the people he helps, but his
secret efforts always end in personal blessing.

While he sips on coffee, he singles out a table or two for blessing.
His blessing conspiracy has paid for the meals of elderly couples, single
parents, and military veterans (sometimes he leaves an unsigned note).
The people try to identify their benefactor, but they don't recognize
George and never assume it could be the coffee-drinking stranger.

He leaves a generous tip as a thank-you to the wait staff for helping him.

George doesn't do this with every meal or on every stop. When he
does, people he's never met leave marveling at his kindness, but he simply
smiles and wonders how God allows him to be so blessed.

God wants us to pay attention to the needs of other people just as
we try to get our own children to recognize the needs they see around
them. Maybe taking our kids on a few secret missions like George's would
be a fun new way to see the kingdom of God. Things done without
expecting anything in return is when God does some of His best work
through and in us.

Father, give us opportunities to be secret agents of the kingdom!

Insecure Much?

There is no fear in love. But perfect love drives out fear,
because fear has to do with punishment. The one
who fears is not made perfect in love.
1 JOHN 4:18 NIV

• •

When it comes to asking a girl out on a date, most guys either hesitate or refuse to ask. They may not admit it, but for most guys there is an absolute fear of rejection. It may be easier to think of what *might have been* instead of facing the potential that she might say no.

Every guy faces insecurity. The most masculine among us will have doubts about whether they're doing life right. A man can be in any decade of life and wonder if he really understands what it means to be a man.

At some point late at night, early in the morning, on the daily commute, or in response to a cutting remark, we collapse inside because we're convinced we don't know what we're doing, and we're afraid others will discover our secret.

We feel like pretenders, and no place seems safe to admit our insecurity.

For those who think that love is a *girly* thing, you should know that love is God's gift to you. His love offers acceptance, invites trust, and is always the safest place to share what's really going on.

God didn't create us without direction. His love for us should make us comfortable in accepting His plan for our lives. God created man, so He knows how we're hardwired.

Real men accept God's love and engage life—fearless.

Father, You alone can make me brave the way Christ was. He was
truly fearless in the life He lived on earth. He faced opposition from
the authorities, questioning from family, doubts from His followers.
But He never wavered in doing what You asked of Him.
Make me more like Your fearless Son!

The Motivation to Follow

*Whom have I in heaven but you? I desire you more than anything
on earth. My health may fail, and my spirit may grow weak,
but God remains the strength of my heart; he is mine forever.*
PSALM 73:25–26 NLT

. . . .

There's almost no kid who doesn't know about the blue-furred creature with a large appetite, Cookie Monster. Maybe you've even said, "Me want cookie," before stuffing one in your mouth alongside your little cookie crunchers. (The Muppet creation's appetite has not been limited to cookies, however. He calls cookies a "sometime snack." He's been seen eating fruit, telephones, and virtually anything that's lying around.)

There are a few lessons we can learn from Cookie Monster. When he's committed to eating a cookie, he doesn't care what people think. When he talks about cookies, he's passionate. His love for cookies is not a short-term interest because cookies have apparently changed his life.

Now, let's look at this idea with a few word changes.

When we're committed to following Jesus, we don't care what people think. When we talk about Jesus, we're passionate. Our love for Jesus is not a short-term interest because Jesus has changed our lives.

The motivation to follow Jesus is tied to how we process His good news. When we understand what Jesus saved us from, what He offers us now, and what He's preparing for our future, we might really begin to see that God's good news is the best news—ever.

*Loving God, You brought the world good news in the gift of Your Son.
I praise You for Your incomparable love, and I want to follow Jesus with
wild abandon, not caring for the opinions of others, but passionate
about You showing the world what You've done for me.*

Changing the Field of Play

GOD's loyal love couldn't have run out, his merciful love couldn't have dried up. They're created new every morning. How great your faithfulness!
LAMENTATIONS 3:22–23 MSG

• •

He was a professional baseball player known more for running than batting. The first four years of his career he was only good enough to be a part-time player. He struck out four times in his first game, and the next few games weren't much better, but he improved.

It wasn't long before Billy Sunday became a fan favorite and an accomplished center fielder for the Chicago White Stockings.

Sunday was one of the most exciting players of his era, one of the fastest runners, but one of the worst hitters. He was an orphan from an early age, and baseball allowed him to cope with life's frustration.

In 1886, Sunday was in downtown Chicago when he stopped by a street mission and met Jesus.

By 1891, he left baseball to preach at a local YMCA for $83 a month. Soon, he would be preaching in towns throughout the United States. Over several decades Sunday would preach in over 300 revivals. More than one hundred million people heard him preach. A million people accepted God's rescue plan.

Billy Sunday was once in an enviable position. Baseball fans loved him. Offers to play were available to him, but the faithfulness of God contained an irresistible grace that drew the baseball player from the playing field to a harvest field.

Sunday found and shared what we all need to discover. God's loyal love is unending. His mercy is refreshing. His faithfulness is beyond awesome.

Good Father, thank You for sharing Your unending love and mercy with us in Christ!

How to Follow God's Will

[God has] already made it plain how to live, what to do. . . .
It's quite simple: Do what is fair and just to your neighbor,
be compassionate and loyal in your love, and don't take
yourself too seriously—take God seriously.
MICAH 6:8 MSG

. . . .

Some Christians want to know God's will because He might have something big for them to do and they don't want to miss it. So in a simple verse like today's reading—that tells us exactly what God wants from us—we might miss it because it doesn't seem to point to a *personalized* plan from God.

Yet we learn God can only trust us with big things when He can trust us with small things first. So, God starts small, the same way we do with our children. It's like He's saying, "You want to know My will for you? Treat your neighbor right. Be compassionate to others and show them My love. Take My Word seriously, and don't be easily offended."

If you think this is easy, try it sometime. In a world where we don't know our neighbors' names, it can be hard to treat them right. At a time when people don't trust each other, it's hard to show compassion. In a place where God's Word is mocked, it can be difficult to take it seriously. In a world where humans live, it's too easy to be offended.

Therein lies the difficulty of your starting place. God's will starts here. Get to a place of faithfulness with these issues, and God will make sure you know what to do next.

Eternal Father, forgive us for being so concerned with our own story
that we forget we are part of Your story! Help us to be faithful in
all that You have revealed already and patient about the rest.

The Success of Failure

Commit your actions to the LORD, and your plans will succeed.
PROVERBS 16:3 NLT

• •

We are confronted with innovative products every day. Many show up on infomercials or shopping channels. Some stores have kiosks dedicated to products we've seen on television. Did you know there are plenty of inventions made by mistake?

Penicillin is a remarkable antibiotic, but it wasn't what Sir Alexander Fleming was trying to invent. He had been working on a wonder drug that cured disease. When that failed, he threw everything away; but looking down at his scientific trash, Fleming noticed a petri dish where mold was consuming bacteria. What he thought was failure was actually a success with a refined perspective.

Then there's the creation of chocolate chip cookies. This, too, was a pretty fantastic failure. The owner of the Toll House Inn needed to make chocolate cookies. Out of baker's chocolate, she used bits of sweetened chocolate thinking they would melt when cooking. Instead, she got tan cookies with defined bits of gooey chocolate goodness. Failure? Any kid in the world knows different!

God's plans for us are always *on purpose* plans, but even if we take a wrong turn somewhere, God can still cause "everything to work together for the good of those who love God and are called according to his purpose for them" (Romans 8:28 NLT).

God never does anything by accident. He loves you intentionally. There's something He planned for you to do. He has made sure you have everything you need to accomplish His plan.

Perspective alters how we define success as well as failure. God can use both.

Father, open my eyes to see success the way You do. For Joseph to get sold into slavery in Egypt must have seemed like a huge disaster at the time, but he remained faithful and both Egypt and Israel were saved! Help me to stop judging success by only what I can see today.

United in Freedom

Those who wait upon GOD get fresh strength.
They spread their wings and soar like eagles, they run
and don't get tired, they walk and don't lag behind.
ISAIAH 40:31 MSG

• •

Perhaps the strongest human connection is between a mother and her children. One of the most devastating moments a mother can experience is to learn that her child was killed in war.

Grace Seibold had been awaiting information about her son. Her hope dissolved in 1918 when news arrived that George was a casualty of World War I.

Grace eventually reached out to other mothers who had lost a child to war. She volunteered in hospitals. She used her pain to become productive.

Ten years later what Grace had initiated came to be known as Gold Star Mothers. These women worked to bring comfort to other families facing similar pain. The organization Grace inspired was named for the gold star placed in the window of military families' homes as a visual reminder of the child who had given everything for their country and a cause.

These mothers understood their son or daughter fought for a better future. Their life was a symbol of national unity. Their memory was reflected in gold stars representing freedom, hope, and gratitude.

Likewise, let us remember our Savior who purchased freedom with His own life. It is the hope that Jesus offers that can inspire those lamenting a loved one lost too early. The strength we need when remembering our lost loved ones is rightfully found in the embracing grace of Jesus.

Father, we honor those who sacrificed their lives for our country's
freedom, but most of all we honor Jesus for His willingness to bring us
freedom by giving His life. We rejoice in the promise of eternal life through
His resurrection, and the gift of freedom from sin by the Holy Spirit.

Things We Think

You will keep in perfect peace all who trust in you,
all whose thoughts are fixed on you!
ISAIAH 26:3 NLT

• •

The things we think often astonish, embarrass, and torture us. We think about things we know are off-limits, and without our permission the thoughts return. And it gets tougher every year as technology gives us access to every kind of wickedness and folly.

When entertaining thoughts that keep us at a distance from God, we may end up acting out in real life what was only supposed to be a private thought.

When we spend time meditating on God's Word, we can have good decisions show up in our lives based on what we *allow* to take up head space.

Hebrews 12:2–3 (MSG) gives some great advice on redirecting and reconnecting your brain to God's plan. "Keep your eyes on Jesus, who both began and finished this race we're in. Study how he did it. Because he never lost sight of where he was headed—that exhilarating finish in and with God—he could put up with anything along the way: Cross, shame, whatever. And now he's there, in the place of honor, right alongside God. When you find yourselves flagging in your faith, go over that story again, item by item, that long litany of hostility he plowed through. That will shoot adrenaline into your souls!"

The story of Jesus is a remedy for bad thinking. We struggle—He helps. We blow it—He forgives. We wander—He encourages focus.

Grow your thought life in God's direction. A full benefits plan is waiting.

Help us, Father, to fill our minds with You and Your great love for us.
Help us to memorize Your words and to meditate on them, nourishing
our souls from what is eternally good. Protect us, and our families, from
the attack of this world; guard our hearts and our minds in Christ Jesus.

Sticks and Stones: Words and Tones

Watch the way you talk. . . . Say only what helps, each word a gift.
EPHESIANS 4:29 MSG

• •

Imagine a father saying to his daughter, "There's no use planning to go to college. It's your younger sister that will make it. She's the smart one." Or maybe, "Looks like you could use a little more time in the gym."

The old phrase "Sticks and stones may break my bones, but words will never hurt me" just isn't true. Words can do as much, if not more, damage than physical injury. The words we speak to our children will always effect a result. Those words can encourage and bring about an open spirit that thrives under our approval, or it can cause an uncertain spirit within our children that will wilt and close when they sense they will never be good enough for us.

Often what dads say is believed by the young ears that hear it spoken. Children can live up, or down, to our expectations.

With words God spoke this world into being. With words we can inspire hope or exile our children to a kingdom of doubt.

We can build our children up with carefully chosen but truthful words. On the other hand, we can tear down with words driven more by emotion or carelessness than fact. Sometimes those wounds last a lifetime. Often they impact the next generation. Occasionally, they will damage the bond between father and child.

A biblical rule of thumb: pay attention to what you say, use words that are helpful, serve each word as a gift that's memorable for all the right reasons.

Father, guard my words! Teach me to encourage with every opportunity and build up my children, not discourage or embitter them. They need You, and I want to bring them closer to You with all my heart.

No Secondhand Story

Do your best to win God's approval as a worker who doesn't need to be ashamed and who teaches only the true message.
2 TIMOTHY 2:15 CEV

• •

Hold on. Dig deep. Work out.

Does the Christian life sometimes sound like that? You might even hear someone say, "Get sweaty for Jesus."

It's true that the apostle Paul refers to the Christian journey as a race, but that's only part of the picture. There are two steps every Christian man should take. The first is love God enough to serve those He loves, starting with our own families. The second is to know enough of God's message that we don't have to be ashamed when someone asks us why we're helping out. It doesn't do much good to lend a hand but then be unable to tell them more about what a relationship with Jesus looks like.

God wants us to teach a true message, not one that's made up or may be a misunderstood hand-me-down secondhand story.

The Bible is where we learn, and we have to balance our walk between helping those who need help and learning more about why we offer help.

In an earlier version of the Bible, we are asked to "study to shew thyself approved of God" (KJV). We don't assume, guess, or even make something up when it comes to answering questions of our faith. We *hold on* to God's hand, we *dig deep* in His Word, and our *spiritual muscles* grow when we really *know* what God said in the Bible.

Study and serve. Learn and give. Memorize and share God's love. He will approve this plan—every time.

God our Father, we want Your approval more than anyone else's. We want to know You more than anyone else. We want to imitate You more than anyone else! Thank You for giving us Your Holy Spirit so that we can hold on, dig deep, and grow in Christ.

Hope: Beyond Wishful Thinking

*The fundamental fact of existence is that this trust in God, this faith,
is the firm foundation under everything that makes life worth living.
It's our handle on what we can't see. The act of faith is what
distinguished our ancestors, set them above the crowd.*
HEBREWS 11:1–2 MSG

• •

If you've ever seen kids writing a Christmas list, then you've seen hope!
While the Bible uses the word *hope* dozens of times, did you know that
it rarely means wishful thinking?

When God tells us to put our hope in Him, He is saying we should
have *no doubts*. If we think of hope as wishful thinking, then doubt can
creep into our thinking, overpowering what should be confident trust.

If we use a phrase from another era, God is asking us to *put all our
eggs in His basket*. In more recent language, we should be *all in*.

Hope is a firm foundation, confident belief, and determined faith.

In our everyday life we can hope an unexpected check comes in the
mail, we can hope our boss doubles our salary, and we can hope our car
will sell for more than we paid for it. In each case, that is little more than
wishful thinking. If we're honest with ourselves, we would admit we have
very little confidence that these things will actually happen.

God's hope should be unshakable, fully dependable, and rooted in
the promises of a loving God.

It is a brave man who hopes in God the way God wants us to hope.
We need to have the intestinal fortitude (guts) to, without doubt, believe
that the God who promised *will* come through.

*Father of all hope and all comfort, help me to be brave and to
hold fast in hope for all that You have promised! Show me where
I can step out in hope and faith and help others to do the same.*

Nothing Escapes His Attention

*"For all that is secret will eventually be brought into
the open, and everything that is concealed will
be brought to light and made known to all."*
LUKE 8:17 NLT

• •

One of the first things you'll notice if you ever have the opportunity to take a hot air balloon ride is how quiet it can be. Because you're blowing with the wind, you don't typically hear it. Because there's no engine, the only noise is the occasional blast of the propane burner to heat the air. Because you're floating on air currents, there's little turbulence.

Equally remarkable are the clear sounds from the earth below. You can hear dogs barking, the excitement of children when they notice you, and the sounds of people calling to you thinking you can't hear them.

While not a perfect picture, this is a bit like God's relationship with us. Nothing escapes His attention—even when He's not recognized. He sees all. He hears all. He knows who we are.

We all learned to play hide-and-seek as kids, but trying to hide from God is no game. Hiding is a lie our adversary asks us to believe is possible, and when we believe it, he comes back to accuse us of being unfaithful to God.

If you've never been in a hot air balloon, it can be hard to imagine what it is like. If you've never really trusted in God, it can be hard to imagine what it's like for God to know all about you while you continue to ignore His presence.

God knows we *will* break His law. He watches, not as a judge, but as one who can compassionately offer forgiveness.

*Father, there is nothing hidden from You. Help us to
remember that it's a blessing to be known so fully by
a loving Father. Rescue us from our own foolishness!*

Stoop Down – Reach Out – Share Burdens

Stoop down and reach out to those who are oppressed.
Share their burdens, and so complete Christ's law.
GALATIANS 6:2 MSG

• •

A friend lost his job. A neighbor lost his health. A coworker lost his promotion. What can you do? How should you respond?

Many men aren't particularly gifted in emotional encounters. If our children get hurt, we often send them to Mom for comfort. If our teen daughter suffers heartbreak, we're often ill equipped for the tears. And don't even think about offering advice!

Maybe we're afraid that if we get too close, the problems we see in the lives of others will become our problems. If things are running smooth in our own lives, we avoid complications.

Following the Golden Rule (Luke 6:31) will find us doing for others the things they could only hope for. Our actions might involve sweat equity, a listening ear, or perhaps a few dollars. We give because God gave. We love because He loves. We forgive because we've been forgiven.

When it feels awkward to share the burden of others, just remember, God's Son, Jesus, became one of us and saw firsthand how we live. Jesus fed the hungry, healed the sick, and taught those He encountered.

If left to ourselves, we are self-preservationists. We want to make sure we have enough, enjoy enough, and play enough. The problems others face are not our problems. Right?

Stoop down. Reach out. Share burdens.

When you do that, you're living in obedience to the God who has never turned His back on you.

Father of compassion, You have borne our burdens through Your own
Son—such a personal way to care for us! Help us to bear the burdens
of those around us with the grace and love You've shown us.

Life's Pop Quizzes

I treasure your word above all else;
it keeps me from sinning against you.
PSALM 119:11 CEV

• •

There's good news: life is an open book test and you have access to all the information you need to answer life's most important questions. There's bad news: the only book you really need is often overlooked.

We live in a world where access to information is not only available, but expected. If we want the latest news, a few deft moves on a smartphone, tablet, or computer and the world is delivered to our screens. We can gain as much information as we want—whenever we want.

We have come to believe that we don't have to be an expert in anything. Why? We can make new discoveries online when needed and then forget them just as quickly—or we store up information that isn't especially important.

God has always wanted us to know what He thinks about the issues that affect us most. We can't act in the way we should if we don't have God's wisdom. We have access to His Word, yet we often stand back and guess when life's pop quizzes show up.

When bad days come and the tests seem the hardest, we should consult God's Word, but our usual response is to complain to the Instructor about the existence of tests.

In school, we review textbooks in preparation for exams, but in real life we tend to view the Bible as an optional text rather than our primary source of wisdom.

We should keep the Bible handy, but as a *treasure* for consultation, not bookshelf ornamentation.

Holy God, though I read and sometimes study the Bible,
I often make excuses for not acting on what I learn.
Help me to listen better to Your voice in Your Word, Father!

The Lord's Army?

No one serving as a soldier gets entangled in civilian affairs,
but rather tries to please his commanding officer.
2 TIMOTHY 2:4 NIV

• •

There's an old hymn that begins, "Onward Christian soldiers, marching as to war, with the cross of Jesus going on before." This has been sung for more than 150 years.

Ironically, the song was originally written for children, and the Salvation Army accepted the song as identifiable with their ministry, but there's been confusion ever since. This hymn is best understood when we consider that it takes dedication, discipleship, and discipline to follow God.

We are God's soldiers when we do what He commands. God's greatest commands are to love God and then everyone else. We only win when we show God's love.

We're to be at peace with people as often as we can (Romans 12:18), serve others (Acts 20:35), and give generously (2 Corinthians 9:7).

Soldiers are trained, soldiers obey, and soldiers love their commanding officer.

The war Christians wage is for the spiritual health of those we know. We protect our own health, nurture our children's health, and introduce Jesus to those we encounter. We press forward because lives are at stake. We should protect and defend but never attack.

The role of a military soldier and a Christian soldier are unique. Sometimes they overlap, but being a soldier for God means your first choice is love.

Father, we know spiritual warfare is our calling.
Grant us the resolve to fight well with the weapons
You provide, and not confuse who the enemy is!

Write on Hearts

Proclaim the Message with intensity; keep on your watch. Challenge, warn, and urge your people. Don't ever quit. Just keep it simple.
2 TIMOTHY 4:2 MSG

• •

Our kids are growing up at the height of the information age. Communication takes place in innumerable ways, through multiple channels, sometimes simultaneously. But as entrenched in technology as they are, most of them still use at least one "ancient" tool.

In the 1880s, John J. Loud wanted something that could be used to mark leather in his shop. He made an effective but crude tool using a ball bearing and ink for his purpose, but early model pens wouldn't be available until the early 1900s. It was postwar 1945 when America finally embraced the new "ballpoint" pen.

Today, millions of pens are produced daily. Billions of words flow from those pens. Trillions of thoughts are explored before writing anything down.

Yet from the first sentence chiseled into stone tablets or scratched onto papyrus to record God's Word, there was a deliberate purpose behind every pen stroke that introduced mankind to the heart of God. If God had waited until the ballpoint pen or the first word processor was available, how many generations would have been without knowledge of the One who created life, love, and forgiveness?

On the other hand, it may be reasonable to believe that today God wants us to use every tool we have at our disposal to share His love. Use a pen, computer, video production, stage presentation, poem, painting, or any other creative way to write His message to the whole world.

God our Father, You are the great Communicator. You've written about Yourself in all creation and in the hearts of mankind. Your Son was called the "Word" because You want to speak to each one of us. Help us to use any tool we can to spread the good news of Your salvation.

He Gives Better Gifts

"Give, and you will receive. Your gift will return to you in full—
pressed down, shaken together to make room for more,
running over, and poured into your lap."
LUKE 6:38 NLT

• •

Everyone loves to get a gift. Kids make lists months in advance of birthdays and Christmas, wives drop hints as anniversaries approach, and leading up to Father's Day, somehow tools, grills, and hammocks make their way into every conversation!

Yep, getting a gift is fun. But, according to Jesus, it's far better to give one. In the Bible, God tells us the following two things about giving: 1) giving is His idea, and 2) we will receive when we give.

Giving can be hard when you never feel like you have enough, when you're trying to save for your future, and because everyone has a selfish streak.

What happens when you give and you don't feel that gift is "returned to you in full"? Let's say you give $100 to your church, but you don't receive $100 in return. You may doubt the accuracy of the verse above.

God always blesses a cheerful giver. He promises to take care of our needs, which means His return gift often goes beyond what we need. Is it possible the gifts we receive from God have never been limited to money?

What if, when we give, we receive a closer relationship with Him? What if our gift is a softened heart, improved outlook, or contentment? What if God's blessing to a generous heart is so much better than mere money that we might be ashamed we ever thought God intended to make us wealthy in the one way that is meaningless in heaven?

God will always give better gifts than He receives.

Father, help us to be cheerful, giving from the heart the
way You offered Christ. Let us not turn away from
becoming like You in the grace of giving.

Interruptions Encouraged

So whenever we are in need, we should come bravely
before the throne of our merciful God. There we will be
treated with undeserved kindness, and we will find help.
HEBREWS 4:16 CEV

• •

When you were in school, the teacher would invite students to ask questions, but at some point you were no longer allowed to ask because you had to take a test or a quiz.

Your parents may have been patient and allowed you to ask questions, but at some point you may have been told, "That's enough now."

In the workplace, your boss may not mind being interrupted for a few questions that help you learn to do your job better, but at some point he has to get back to his own work.

Try to think of someone—anyone—who likes being interrupted. Is it hard to identify this superhuman?

God is the only one who doesn't mind His children asking as many questions, they want. He never objects to interruptions. He never asks us to be more considerate. What God actually tells us is to be brave when we come to Him, expect kindness we don't deserve, and find the help we need.

God is more than patient with our interruptions. Why? Maybe it's because when we're willing to be brave enough to come to Him, we are telling Him we are interested in knowing His heart, plan, and purpose for our lives.

Relationships begin with conversation. Interrupt God whenever you need to. The end result is a closeness that will never be found trying to do things on your own—without His help.

Father, I praise You for Your constant availability to me! You enjoy my
interruptions and my boldness in Christ! Your interest in me cannot be
lessened, and I thank You for being the most patient Father of all.

Beyond Life Hacks

While you are in the world, you will have to suffer.
But cheer up! I have defeated the world.
JOHN 16:33 CEV

• •

Have you used a *life hack*? These hacks (or tips) give you an opportunity to use items you probably already own to make certain jobs easier.

With the right life hack you can use a waffle maker to create a panini sandwich, a clothespin to hold a nail when hammering, duct tape to open a difficult jar, or toothpaste to clear up your headlight covers.

There aren't many life hacks for things like a rebellious child, a struggling marriage, a job in jeopardy, or a habit you can't break.

Difficult circumstances are common to all, and the best wisdom on how to get through it seems useless. We try ignoring it, wishing it away, and confronting it head-on. We might be surprised that in some cases none of our attempts at making life easier seem to work.

One universal truth to remember is that *life is hard*. Certainly there are enjoyable parts, but there are plenty of things we just seem to endure. Rather than take this knowledge and become pessimistic, we should remember that we can always draw close to the One who has overcome or defeated the world.

When the apostle Paul struggled with a hard life, God said, "My kindness is all you need. My power is strongest when you are weak" (2 Corinthians 12:9 CEV).

Admittedly, men tend to be self-sufficient, action oriented, and often reluctant to ask for help. God wants us to realize we should ask Him for help because He's the only one who is perfectly reliable.

Jesus, You declared that in this world we would face trouble but that You have overcome the world. Let this truth sink deep into our souls today! There are no shortcuts to fixing our problems. But we have Your promises and Your Spirit, which are far more valuable!

The Job of Being Dad

*They say—again, quite rightly—that there is only one God the Father,
that everything comes from him, and that he wants us to live for him.*
1 CORINTHIANS 8:6 MSG

• •

Bring up the subject of fathers and you discover those who can recall with great fondness the role he had in their lives. There are also those who live with painful memories of an absent or even unknown father.

Not all men take the job of being a dad seriously. If you're a dad, you may be following the pattern of a great dad, maybe even breaking the cycle of a father who just wasn't engaged in his role, or you might be repeating his behavior.

For some men, the idea of viewing God as their Father seems less than ideal. They know what their dad was like, and if God is anything like their memory, then the term *Father* has negative emotional connections.

When you take the time to look at the attributes of God, you find that He is loving, merciful, kind, all-knowing, unchanging, faithful, honorable, holy, and forgiving, just to name a few.

If that sounds different than your father, then maybe getting to know God can help change your understanding of what it looks like from God's perspective to be a father.

If you find that list impressive, then you should know that God has given you a list of traits you can rely on, and He still wants you to know Him as Father.

*There is no greater comfort than knowing You, Father! You are
perfect in all of Your ways and loving beyond any expectation.
You made us part of Your family through the gift of Jesus Christ.
Help us as fathers to be like You and to model You to our children.*

Acquitted

"Anyone who trusts in [Jesus] is acquitted; anyone who refuses to trust him has long since been under the death sentence without knowing it. And why? Because of that person's failure to believe in the one-of-a-kind Son of God when introduced to him."
JOHN 3:18 MSG

• •

Frank R. Stockton's classic short story, "The Lady, or the Tiger," follows a young man who is unworthy to marry the princess but has fallen in love with her, thus breaking the king's law.

The king had his own method of determining guilt and innocence. Any individual accused of crimes against the king would face an arena where death could result. The accused entered the arena facing two doors. If the accused was a man, there would be a beautiful woman that he was to marry behind one door and a savage and hungry tiger behind the other. He alone could make the choice between doors. That choice determined his fate.

Since this was actually little more than a game of chance, there was no reliable way to determine innocence or guilt. Nothing more than a flip of the coin.

Aren't you glad God has a more clearly defined sense of justice?

With God we enter His proverbial arena where we're simply asked if we're guilty of sin. Our only truthful answer has to be yes. God will need to know how we'll pay for our guilt. In His court there's only one correct answer. *Jesus* paid the guilt price for our sin. We could choose to try to pay the price on our own, but that choice separates us from the love of God and ends in death.

Choose Jesus—discover real life.

Merciful Father, I am so glad to have You as my Judge and Jesus as my Savior! Let me bring the truth of this good news to those around me, starting in my own household.

In Constant Communication

But the Holy Spirit will come and help you, because the Father will send the Spirit to take my place. The Spirit will teach you.
JOHN 14:26 CEV

• •

It ain't your typical family camping trip when the reality television show offers two folks the opportunity to spend a couple of days outdoors. They venture off alone but are in constant two-way communication with a survival expert who will help them get through circumstances that are way outside their comfort zone.

The survival expert knows how to get the contestants from the starting point to a celebrated ending. He knows how to help them get food and water. All that's really needed is a contestant willing to follow directions—no matter how strange the instructions sound.

Some contestants start strong but refuse to follow instructions. Others seem to struggle with the circumstances they face, but they listen and do exactly what they're told.

Those who finish have an incredible story to share; they're more capable when facing future challenges and are able to encourage others who struggle.

Christians are asked to participate in adventures we can never finish on our own. We need help. First Corinthians 10:13 (NLT) says, "The temptations in your life are no different from what others experience. And God is faithful. He will not allow the temptation to be more than you can stand. When you are tempted, he will show you a way out so that you can endure."

God will send His Holy Spirit to give us the guidance we need to do every hard thing we face. He is with us—from start to finish.

Father, some days I confess it feels more like survival than anything else. But I take You at Your word when You say You will never leave me alone. I thank You for your Holy Spirit and ask You to help me to listen better to Your inner leading.

Restless, and Hating It

Why am I discouraged? Why am I restless? I trust you!
And I will praise you again because you help me.
PSALM 42:5 CEV

• •

Have you ever had feelings of restlessness? You feel like you should do something, but you don't know what. You can't sleep well and you don't know why. You feel like you have a deadline, but you don't know when.

There are two primary reasons why men experience restlessness. The first is because they know they're in a bad place where poor choice or discontent are their best friends. The second is when they recognize they're in the wrong spiritual location.

There is a restlessness that results in a downward spiral, and there is a restlessness that results in a U-turn.

Feelings of unrest can leave us with plenty of room for self-reflection. Identifying the reasons why we're restless can help us determine where we're headed next, and why.

Restlessness usually means we're not where we should be and suggests the need to relocate our heads, hearts, and hopes.

God can send unrest into our lives when we get too comfortable in circumstances God doesn't want for us in a place where we've stayed too long.

Restlessness can be God's invitation to a new adventure, for yourself and your family.

Confusion, apprehension, and *depression* may all be words that could be used to describe that godly unrest that screams, *Move.*

God's call can be ignored, but the restlessness will not go away until you answer the call.

When you feel restless, and we all will, it's an incredible opportunity to follow God's plan.

Father, we can only find true rest in You.

The Three Investments

*"Above all and before all, do this: Get Wisdom!
Write this at the top of your list: Get Understanding!"*
PROVERBS 4:7 MSG

• •

Everything we do requires an investment of time, energy, or talents. Work, family, community, personal interests. Some we take on willingly, and others reluctantly.

In the demand for the limited resources of our time, energy, and talents, some might consider it a waste to help someone who has no way to return the favor.

If you believe that the best use of these three investments is for monetary or personal gain, then it becomes easy to believe that helping others is a waste. However, if you believe that God has given you these three investments to use for His purposes, then helping others is not only a good use, but perhaps the best use of your personal resources. To put this in perspective, understand that God invests everything He has in *relationships*. He is a *Person* and so all relationships matter to Him—so much so that He says the way we treat others, especially those in need, is the way we treat Him!

First Timothy 6:17–19 (MSG) is a pretty good overview of how God looks at our investments. "Tell those rich in this world's wealth to quit being so full of themselves and so obsessed with money, which is here today and gone tomorrow. Tell them to go after God, who piles on all the riches we could ever manage—to do good, to be rich in helping others, to be extravagantly generous. If they do that, they'll build a treasury that will last, gaining life that is truly life."

*Father God, You are the reason we have relationships
in the first place—they reflect You in our lives.*

In the Presence of Greatness

"Show respect to the aged."
LEVITICUS 19:32 MSG

• •

Route 66 covers nearly 2,500 miles of byways, hills, and history. Many still consider it the *Mother Road*.

This highway is the tangible memory of the days of large cars and cross-country adventure when travelers were met with hospitality, full service gas stations, drive-in theaters, and diners.

Traveling this road made it to bucket lists before there were bucket lists.

In the autumn of 1936, the highway was put into service. Enjoying the open spaces of the Heartland turned into a national pastime.

In the 1950s, the Interstate was introduced to America's landscape. Traffic began moving away from the time-honored route.

Today, sections of Route 66 are rededicated to the culture of the road. Classic diners have been restored. Many feel an invitation to return to a simpler time in America's history.

In 1985, Route 66 was set aside in favor of faster travel on the Interstate. Some states have made portions of the old highway national historical sites. The legacy of Route 66 lives on.

There's a similar sense of honor that God calls us to offer to those who've lived longer than we have. The wisdom learned or obtained by these men and women is often overlooked and underappreciated. Maybe a parent or grandparent, an aunt or uncle; perhaps someone you've seen at church—the stories are there for the asking. Invite them to share their stories, triumphs, and even struggles.

Honor the wisdom of the aging because God commanded it. This gift of honor brings long-term blessings.

Holy God, if it is Your will, one day I will
be the elder someone needs to listen to.

The Plan, Goal, and Purpose

*Keep your eyes on Jesus, who both began and finished this race we're in.
Study how he did it. Because he never lost sight of where he was headed—
that exhilarating finish in and with God—he could put up with anything
along the way: Cross, shame, whatever. And now he's there, in the place
of honor, right alongside God. When you find yourselves flagging in your
faith, go over that story again, item by item, that long litany of hostility
he plowed through. That will shoot adrenaline into your souls!*
HEBREWS 12:2–3 MSG

• •

Keep your eye on the prize. Get your head into the game. Press on. Play
with purpose.

Every single thing that requires a plan, completes a goal, and captures
the purpose of the heart requires focus. We teach this to our kids, but
do we forget it in our own lives?

When a runner is *beyond* tired, it's the finish line that inspires them
to push forward and finish strong. When a singer has been invited to
perform their first solo, it's the audience that inspires courage. When an
entrepreneur comes up with a brilliant idea, it's the launch of their product
that gives them their first real sense of hope.

There will be days when the Christian life is hard. Our adversary will
distract us and offer the equivalent of a recliner, detour, or false promise.
He won't care if he's able to totally ruin our lives. All he really wants is to
shift our focus.

Keep the focus on Jesus. Learn who He is, how He lived, and what
He wants.

Feeling weary? Spend time with His story. Regain your focus, get
your second wind, and press on.

*O eternal God! Help me to focus my efforts, my hopes, and my life on Jesus
alone! In Him I have life and freedom from the distractions of this world.
Be my life, O Lord, and my joy. Teach me to put off the worthless things
that crowd You out and to run with all my strength the race set by You.*

A Place to Sit

And seeing the multitudes, He went up on a mountain,
and when He was seated His disciples came to Him.
Then He opened His mouth and taught them.
MATTHEW 5:1–2 NKJV

• •

When we think of the Sermon on the Mount, we picture Jesus (as Hollywood has coached us) perched on a high rock up in the hills, teaching the multitudes—or walking through tall grass on the mountainside, reciting the Beatitudes as He maneuvers among the masses congregated there. But scripture says He walked away from the crowd, headed into the hills, and found a place to sit. When His closest followers came to Him, He taught them. This is a picture of intimate impartation to a few, not a scene with stage lights, microphones, and a megachurch multitude.

Evangelist Billy Graham spent a long life in the spotlight, and millions have responded to his presentation of the Gospel. Yet, if he could live his life over, he'd do a few things differently. "For one thing," he said, "I would speak less and study more, and I would spend more time with my family."

Men too often long for the soapbox and the spotlight. We want to hear the applause and the "amen." But Jesus looks for faithfulness in little things (Luke 16:10). He calls us to feed our own households and teach our own children first and foremost (Matthew 24:45; Ephesians 6:4; 1 Timothy 5:8). Whether or not we're called to speak to the many, we must often step away from the crowds and find a place to sit with the few in our lives who matter most.

God, let us not overlook the very ones in our own house that You
have given us to serve. They are our first priority in Your kingdom
and the disciples we can most influence. When, and if, You call
us to sacrifice our time with them for something else, let us
trust that You will care for them in our absence.

Meek Ain't Weak

"Blessed are the meek, for they shall inherit the earth."
MATTHEW 5:5 NKJV

• •

History trumpets the names of men who have tried to conquer the world: Genghis Khan, Alexander the Great, Napoleon Bonaparte, Julius Caesar, Attila the Hun, Charlemagne, Adolf Hitler. As you read their names and recall their character, does the word *meek* come to mind? Probably not.

Had they been men of gentle temperament, they would not have so violently tread so much turf and shed so much blood. And to what end? A grave beneath the earth they sought to rule!

Jesus said, "The meek will inherit the earth"—not the militant, but the *meek!*

Meek isn't weak. Meek is gentle, mild, and humble—but not weak.

Jesus said of Himself, "I am meek and lowly in heart" (Matthew 11:29 KJV). Was He weak? No way! Physically, emotionally, spiritually, intellectually, and relationally, Jesus was a man's man. Scripture notes His growth in wisdom and stature even as a teen (Luke 2:52). Dean Plumptre wrote, "The Boy grew into youth, and the young Man into manhood, and his purity and lowliness. . .drew even then the hearts of all men." As a man, He endured the torture of crucifixion with astounding self-control (see the Gospel accounts). Then He rose from the dead! Meek ain't weak.

A strong man must be meek and gentle, for otherwise he might harm those smaller and weaker than he is.

One day Jesus will create a new heaven and a new earth (Revelation 21:1–3) as the inheritance of the meek, a gift for the followers of Jesus.

Father, You are our only strength, and You display it when we trust in You rather than our own power. Even if we could gain the whole world by might, it would mean nothing to Your kingdom. Help us to practice the meekness and the patient confidence of Your Son.

A Hungry Man

"Blessed are those who hunger and thirst
for righteousness, for they shall be filled."
MATTHEW 5:6 NKJV

• •

Jesus understood the hardships of life from His childhood in first-century Palestine. When He talked about hungering and thirsting, He knew what that meant and so did His audience.

In Jesus' day, the daily wage was equivalent to three cents; nobody got fat on that. Jewish working men—never far from the borderline of real hunger or actual starvation—ate meat once a week. And thirst was worse; few besides the Romans had water in their homes.

In reality, this beatitude is a stark challenge: Do you want righteousness as much as a starving man wants food or a parched man needs water? How intense is your desire for God, for His goodness and glory?

To the privileged, hunger and thirst can become idolatrous. Desiring food we don't need, eating when we've had enough (more than enough), we become gluttons. But hunger and thirst for righteousness is a safe appetite, a holy appetite, a right appetite. We were created for righteousness.

Saint Augustine, in his *Confessions*, wrote, "God, you have made us for yourself, and our hearts are restless till they find their rest in you."

Jesus said, "I am the bread of life. Whoever comes to me will never go hungry, and whoever believes in me will never be thirsty (John 6:35 NIV). " 'Man shall not live on bread alone, but on every word that comes from the mouth of God' " (Matthew 4:4 NIV).

Only God and His Word can fill us and refuel us to follow Jesus.

Father, You have made us to feast on You alone for our spiritual food!
Jesus said His flesh was "true" bread and His blood "true" drink,
and by feeding on Him we would never go away hunger or thirsty.
Help us come to Your table daily to feed on what leads to eternal life!

Mercy Me

"Blessed are the merciful, for they shall obtain mercy."
MATTHEW 5:7 NKJV

• •

Second Corinthians 1:3 (NKJV) says that God is the "Father of mercies." Mercy is one of God's attributes, given to us in Christ so that we may extend it to others—even to our enemies. To be like our Father, we must be merciful (Luke 6:35–36).

A criminal is shown mercy when his sentence is shortened. A prisoner of war is shown mercy when he is treated humanely. The fallen gladiator in the Roman Colosseum was shown mercy when the dignitaries in the box seats gave a thumbs-up to let him live.

We extend mercy when we bless those who curse us, pray for those who persecute us, and do good to those who do us wrong (Matthew 5:44). We show our children mercy when we patiently give them another chance at something they've failed (or refused) to do. Mercy, like grace, is undeserved favor, something extended to others who may not merit it but need it.

Though we deserve judgment for our sin, God's great mercy has given us new birth instead, and a living hope through the resurrection of Jesus Christ (1 Peter 1:3). Thus we show mercy and forgiveness to others (Ephesians 4:32).

Saint Augustine, an early church father who received the mercy of God through a dramatic conversion experience, wrote: "Two works of mercy set a man free: forgive and you will be forgiven. And give and you will receive." We could call this "the law of divine reciprocity." In other words, "You reap what you sow."

Do you need mercy? Give mercy.

God of mercy, in Christ You have given me what I could never achieve for myself—salvation! Help me this day, Father, to extend Your mercy to others in my life as a testimony to what You've done for me.

Peacemakers

"Blessed are the peacemakers, for they shall be called sons of God."
MATTHEW 5:9 NKJV

• •

Girls play "house"; boys play "war": a politically incorrect truism, but the fact is that men and women are wired differently. Men just aren't natural peacemakers.

Samuel Colt, inventor of the first revolving cylinder handgun once said, "The good people in this world are very far from being satisfied with each other, and my [guns] are the best peacemaker." When Colt died from a sudden illness in 1862, his wife took over the gun business and developed the famous Colt .45, still known today by its nickname, The Peacemaker. Many a frontier sheriff carried this gun in his role as peacekeeper.

When Jesus said, "Blessed are the peacemakers," He didn't have guns in mind. His peace doesn't come with gun in hand but with love in heart. The love of God disarms the heart of man. The kindness, forbearance, patience, and goodness of God lead us to repentance (Romans 2:4). Jesus shed His blood to make peace between God and humankind—and between man and man (Colossians 1:20).

As ambassadors of the Prince of Peace, we don't "walk softly and carry a big stick" (as US President Teddy Roosevelt once described his foreign policy). We simply walk softly, for as Solomon wrote: "A soft answer turns away wrath, but a harsh word stirs up anger" (Proverbs 15:1 NKJV). Christ makes His appeal of peace through us as we implore others to make their peace with God (2 Corinthians 5:20). In this way, like the Prince of Peace Himself, we will be called sons of God.

Father, You are the Author of peace between You and me, peace between me and others, and peace with myself. How wonderful and unfathomable and good are all Your ways, O Lord!

Improbable Joy

*"Blessed are those who are persecuted for righteousness' sake,
for theirs is the kingdom of heaven."*
MATTHEW 5:10 NKJV

• •

Saint Augustine, fifth-century bishop and theologian, wrote, "From Abel to the end of times, the people of God will always suffer persecution on their journey through time." Paul told Timothy that everyone who desires to live right in Christ Jesus will be persecuted (2 Timothy 3:12). Church statistician David Barrett estimates that around seventy million Christians have died for the faith since the stoning of Stephen. In our own day, martyrdom and persecutions are at an unprecedented high. Globally—even in America—persecution of Christians is rising as an antichrist mentality seats itself in the boardrooms, newsrooms, classrooms, war rooms, rest rooms, and throne rooms of our world's most influential institutions.

It appears (if we have eyes to see) that we are living in the day that Jesus spoke of when He told His disciples, "You will be hated by all nations because of me" (Matthew 24:9 NIV).

So what does Jesus command us to do? "Rejoice and be exceedingly glad" (Matthew 5:12 NKJV).

What?! We'd have to be crazy to get happy about persecution—but maybe we know something that our persecutors don't, that no matter what happens to us down here we've got heaven! The kingdoms of this earth will all fall, but the kingdom of heaven will last forever. An incredible reward awaits us there. "Therefore, my beloved brethren, be steadfast, immovable, always abounding in the work of the Lord, knowing that your labor is not in vain in the Lord" (1 Corinthians 15:58 NKJV).

*Good Father, if You count me worthy to suffer for the sake of Christ,
rather than the things common to all men, then let me find joy in
knowing You have blessed me as You did Jesus, my Savior!*

"You Fool!"

"But I say to you that whoever is angry with his brother
without a cause shall be in danger of the judgment."
MATTHEW 5:22 NKJV

• •

Jerry's mother left him when he was young, and now they were separated by four decades and several hundred miles. When Richard asked if Jerry was still in contact with his mother, Jerry replied, "That fool? I hope I never talk to her again!" She was "guilty" according to the anger and judgment in Jerry's heart, and he had never let her out of his interior prison. "I can't forgive her," he said.

"Yes, you can," Richard countered.

"You're right," Jerry admitted, "but I will not!"

Who was really in prison? Jerry was! His mother had long since asked forgiveness for her foolishness, and she was not in her son's prison—he was. Locked up with his anger, it had even eaten away at his body. In his fifties, he was crippled by years of degenerative rheumatoid arthritis. Anger can fester. It can kill. Ecclesiastes 7:9 (NKJV) says, "Do not hasten in your spirit to be angry, for anger rests in the bosom of fools." The Contemporary English Version says, "Only fools. . .hold a grudge." Ephesians 4:26–27 (CEV) exhorts, "Don't get so angry that you sin. Don't go to bed angry and don't give the devil a chance."

Who is the fool, Jerry or his mother? And who is more in danger of judgment?

What do *you* do with your anger? Have you forgiven others as Christ forgave you? "The hour is coming," wrote Dietrich Bonhoeffer, "when we shall meet the Judge face to face, and then it will be too late."

Father, help us to release anything we have against
anyone—especially family—so that we can face You
in our quiet moments without the stain of bitterness.

Cut It Out!

*"If your right eye causes you to sin, pluck it out and cast if from you;
for it is more profitable for you that one of your members perish,
than for your whole body to be cast into hell."*
MATTHEW 5:29 NKJV

• •

In the sci-fi thriller *World War Z*, a zombie pandemic threatens the world. Only one thing stands in the way of the annihilation of humanity: a courageous team led by a United Nations investigator (played by Brad Pitt). When a woman is bitten by a zombie, Pitt cuts off her hand to save her from the infection that will turn her into a mindless, rampaging maniac. It was better that her hand perish than for her whole body to live the hellish existence of a zombie.

But in the admonition to pluck out the eye that causes sin, Jesus isn't telling us to dismember ourselves! That would be a deluded and tragic interpretation of His words. He is using such strong, violent imagery to tell us how critical it is that we "cut sin off at its root."

If your eye causes you to sin—if you are looking at things you shouldn't look at—deal radically and decisively with the situation. Don't let sin have any advantage in your life even through a normal channel. Be ruthless with sin—it's our enemy and the enemy of our families.

Confession and accountability to another brother can often cut temptation at the roots. Be proactive with areas that sin has taken advantage of. It's hard to come clean—but look at the alternative!

*O God, You sent Your own Son to die for our sins—how can
we then take sin so lightly? We do not understand the real
gravity of sin; we do not know its real cost. Teach us to hate
any sin that would ruin our chance to come closer to You!*

Hitched

*"But I say to you that whoever divorces his wife for any reason
except sexual immorality causes her to commit adultery."*
MATTHEW 5:32 NKJV

. . . .

"This the place where a fella gits a license to git hitched?" a young man
asked.

"Yessir," answered the county clerk, looking up from his paperwork.

"Well," said the young man. "Make me up a certificate so that Peter
Brown can marry Suzanny Summers."

"Are you Peter Brown?" the clerk asked.

"I am Peter Brown," declared the young man.

"Is the young lady of age?"

Peter hesitated. "No. . .she ain't!"

"Oh! Then you have her father's permission to marry her?"

"Well, you can bet I do!" said the young man, moving over to the
window. "See thet old man a-settin' in the back of thet pick-up, shotgun
'cross his lap? That's her pa!"

Shotgun weddings are few these days, but once hitched, maybe we
need a little buckshot nudge to stay hitched. For believers, the nudge is
God's Word itself. "I hate divorce!" God said (Malachi 2:16 NLT). "Therefore
what God has joined together, let no one separate," Jesus commanded
concerning marriage (Matthew 19:6 NIV).

"Till death do us part" should not be a death wish for our spouse
but a lifetime commitment to exemplify the everlasting faithfulness of the
One who laid down His life for us (His "bride") at Calvary.

*God our Father, only You know all that goes on inside a marriage.
Show us how to serve and to love our spouse and model
a Christlike attitude in front of our watching children.*

Toothless

*"You have heard that it was said,
'An eye for an eye and a tooth for a tooth.'"*
MATTHEW 5:38 NKJV

• •

An eye for an eye and a tooth for a tooth was a limitation to revenge, not a "right" as some have used it. Rather than suing the restaurant for a million dollars if a waiter spills hot coffee in your lap, you spill hot coffee on his lap in return.

The human heart, especially in kids, needs limits. If we are honest with ourselves, we'd all pay back *more* for every injury, not just equal. This is a hard thing to teach a child, but if it doesn't get addressed early, it will only escalate later on.

The alternative—to "turn the other cheek"—takes time for kids to learn. Maturity in understanding requires patience. Especially since turning the other cheek may be required over and over. When Peter tried to get Jesus to applaud the idea of forgiving his brother a grand total of seven times, Jesus said, "Nope, not seven, but seventy times seven" (Matthew 18:22). In other words, again and again and again. . .as often as forgiveness is needed.

Payback, retaliation, vengeance: it's not ours to dole out. Not at all. It belongs to the only One who is truly just (Romans 12:19).

"To sum up," in the words of Peter (who finally got it), "all of you be harmonious, sympathetic, brotherly, kindhearted, and humble in spirit; not returning evil for evil or insult for insult, but giving a blessing instead; for you were called for the very purpose that you might inherit a blessing" (1 Peter 3:8–9 NASB).

Forgiving Father, help us to model real forgiveness in front of our children. Allow us to demonstrate that turning the other cheek is not only possible, but brings peace in our walk with Christ. Help them to learn that retaliation robs us of a chance to grow closer to Jesus.

"Inspiteful" Prayer

"Pray for those who spitefully use you and persecute you."
MATTHEW 5:44 NKJV

. . . .

David prayed, "Break the teeth in their mouths, O God; LORD, tear out the fangs of those lions! Let them vanish like water that flows away; when they draw the bow, let their arrows fall short. May they be like a slug that melts away as it moves along, like a stillborn child that never sees the sun" (Psalm 58:6–8 NIV).

Why can't I pray against my enemies like that? They deserve it, don't they? It's a terribly degrading thing to be bullied, picked on, and singled out for spiteful abuse, especially as a kid! We all hate a bully. When we're being abused, we'd like to pay a bit of it back (with interest), but Jesus says, "Don't. That's My job. Your job is to pray that I don't *have* to pay it back."

Jesus prayed from the cross for the men who nailed Him there, for the men gambling for His clothes at His feet, for the men who delivered Him to the Romans and stood gloating, cursing, and mocking Him at His crucifixion. He prayed, "Father, forgive them!"

Stephen, the first Christian martyr, prayed for his executioners when their stones knocked him to his knees, "Lord, do not hold this sin against them!"

When we pray for our enemies, at least two things usually happen: 1) our own hearts change as we become more like Christ, and 2) God hears our prayers! Pray that your enemies will see God's goodness and love, repent of their sin, and be brought near to God (Romans 2:4).

Lord, how hard it is sometimes to pray for people who mistreat us!
And even harder if they are mistreating our kids! Help us to have
the faith it takes to bring You into these tough situations, and see
Your glory overwhelm our own desires for revenge!

Vain Repetitions

"They think that they will be heard for their many words."
MATTHEW 6:7 NKJV

• •

Hindus pray mantras, chanted repeatedly, believing they will move the gods to hear and act on their behalf.

Buddhists have prayer wheels with mantras written on the outside of a cylindrical spindle. They believe that spinning the wheel will have the same effect as orally reciting the prayers over and over. The more the wheel turns, the greater the effect of the "prayer." They aren't looking for answers to personal requests. They believe their repetitious chants draw them closer to an inner sense of wholeness called nirvana: a state of perfect peace.

We are not to pray like that. Jesus offers the only perfect peace (John 14:27; Isaiah 26:3). Praying over and over again will not conjure the peace that only comes when we consciously cast our cares upon Him. In the words of a treasured hymn: "What a friend we have in Jesus, all our sins and griefs to bear. What a privilege to carry everything to God in prayer."

Though He already knows our needs, God wants to hear from us. He's a Father desiring relationship with His children. We would never look down on our children's prayers because they weren't long or eloquent enough! How much more does God love our simple, heartfelt prayers? Jesus said, "Come to me, all you who are weary and burdened, and I will give you rest. Take my yoke upon you and learn from me, for I am gentle and humble in heart, and you will find rest for your souls" (Matthew 11:28–29 NIV).

God hears His children, not because of their many words, but because they come to Him to learn from Him, to walk and talk with Him. He cares (1 Peter 5:6–7).

Father, You hear the prayer of our souls with the generous heart of a Father. Thank You. Thank You.

Two Masters

"You cannot serve God and mammon."
MATTHEW 6:24 NKJV

• •

Benedict Arnold was a bold, brilliant field commander. In 1775, he invaded Canada, nearly making it the fourteenth American state. In 1777, he won the Battle of Saratoga, a victory which reversed the Continental Army's losing streak and convinced the French to come to the aid of the colonies. But Arnold was a self-seeking man. Accused of corruption, he once faced court martial for putting military funds in his own pocket. When a battle wound sidelined him to garrison duty, he bitterly brooded on the under-appreciation of his martial genius.

Desire for riches and honor moved Arnold to believe he'd do better as an officer in the enemy's army! While commanding West Point, he systematically weakened the fort's defenses and drained its supplies. At the same time, he started moving his assets from Connecticut to England. For switching sides, he asked the British for money and a major general's commission. But no man can serve two masters—for he'll cling to the one while despising the other. In the end, the traitor earned only the disdain of both Americans and Brits—and his true master (money) could not save him from poor health. He died in London at the age of sixty.

We would be wise to learn from Arnold's foolishness and to teach our children to avoid seeking money for money's sake. From their first allowance to their first job, teach them to honor God with the first fruits of their income. "For the love of money is the root of all kinds of evil. And some people, craving money, have wandered from the true faith and pierced themselves with many sorrows," but "godliness with contentment is itself great wealth" (1 Timothy 6:10, 6 NLT).

Generous Father, You give us all good things. You provide
for us as we seek what really matters—Your kingdom.
Show Yourself to our children as their Provider, and help
them to trust You with every dollar that comes their way.

Splinter Inspection

"And why do you look at the speck in your brother's eye,
but do not consider the plank in your own eye?"
MATTHEW 7:3 NKJV

• •

The tattoo on his arm read "Only God can judge me." His lips spouted judgments about everything and everybody else around him. Jesus said, "Don't judge, and you won't be judged." But He also said, "Judge right judgment. Stop judging by mere appearances, but instead judge correctly" (John 7:24). So. . .we're allowed to judge if we do it right? Yeah, but we gotta do the *Judge-right Two-step* first: 1) take the log out of your own eye, and 2) then help your brother with the splinter in his eye.

Got dust (or an eyelash) in your eye? It hurts, you blink, a tear rolls. You want to rub it! Get a mirror, look close—lift the eyelid to see what you can see. Eyeball to eyeball, that little hair looks (and feels) like a Popsicle stick! It's a matter of perspective—and that's Jesus' point.

And it's always harder for the young. When the crowd wanted to stone a woman caught in sin, Jesus challenged them to throw a stone *only if they had never sinned.* The result was "those who heard began to go away one at a time, the older ones first." (John 8:9 NIV).

"If someone is caught in a sin. . .restore that person gently. But watch yourselves"—examine yourselves—"or you also may be tempted" (Galatians 6:1 NIV). The Message paraphrases it like this, "If someone falls into sin, forgivingly restore him, saving your critical comments for yourself. You might be needing forgiveness before the day's out."

"But if we judged ourselves rightly, we would not be judged" (1 Corinthians 11:31 NASB). Taking time to learn about ourselves before God is critical, and especially for our children.

Good Father, help me to be patient with all, especially my own children,
and recognize opportunities to show them Your gentleness.

The Golden Rule

"Whatever you want men to do to you, do also to them."
MATTHEW 7:12 NKJV

• •

These words capture the essence of the Christian life—in every situation treat others as we ourselves want to be treated. This is indeed the "Golden Rule" of civilized humanity.

Tragically, the human heart is anything but golden. It is, in fact, deceitful above all things (Jeremiah 17:9) and therefore incapable—apart from God—of living by this rule. It rewrites the rule to say: "Do to others *before* they do to you," anticipating the betrayal of other hearts. It says, "Do to others as they *have done* to you," as payback. These, sadly, come naturally to all of us—just watch kids on a playground.

But Solomon wrote, "Whoever digs a pit will fall into it; if someone rolls a stone, it will roll back on them" (Proverbs 26:27 NIV). Any act against anyone will have its eventual payback, because "God cannot be mocked. A man reaps what he sows. Whoever sows to please their flesh, from the flesh will reap destruction; whoever sows to please the Spirit, from the Spirit will reap eternal life" (Galatians 6:7–8 NIV).

The Spirit enables us to obey the Golden Rule, so "let us not become weary in doing good, for at the proper time we will reap a harvest if we do not give up. Therefore, as we have opportunity, let us do good to all people, especially to those who belong to the family of believers" (Galatians 6:9–10 NIV).

How do we define "good"? Apply the Golden Rule: what we think would be good for us, do the same for others.

Jesus, You alone truly lived the Golden Rule. And You did it in the face of violent rejection and hatred. Help us to take on Your life and Your strength that we can imitate Your meekness and humility.

Rock Solid

"Whoever hears these sayings of Mine, and does them. . .
[is like] a wise man who built his house on the rock."
MATTHEW 7:24 NKJV

• •

In 2011, Hurricane Irene poured out her tears on Lancaster County, raising the Conestoga River higher than most folks have ever seen it. In the city of Lancaster, a new biking trail ran along the river, separated from the water by a rugged rail fence. When Irene sent the river running down that trail, its waters carried away most of the rails and fence posts. Only a few hardy posts were still standing when the river receded at last. Those posts had been secured in a concrete section of the path where folks could park to access the trail. The other posts had been installed only in the soil beside the path.

When Jesus finished His Sermon on the Mount, He told a parable about two houses: one with a foundation on rock, the other with a foundation on sand. When Hurricane Irene (or one of her great-grandmothers, anyway) came whistling through, both those houses took a bad beating. The rains fell, the floods came, and the winds blew. When the storm was gone, only one house was still standing—the house built on rock.

"Anyone who listens to my teaching and follows it is wise," said Jesus, "like a person who builds a house on solid rock. . . . But anyone who hears my teaching and doesn't obey it is foolish, like a person who builds a house on sand" (Matthew 7:24, 26 NLT).

There's always a storm coming. Build on rock.

Father, help me to put Your words into action today. Let me build on a
solid foundation for the sake of my family and those I serve. Above all,
strengthen me to be a good and faithful son to You today and forever.

Who Are You Encouraging?

"Martha, Martha," the Lord answered, "you are worried and upset about many things, but few things are needed—or indeed only one. Mary has chosen what is better, and it will not be taken away from her."
LUKE 10:41–42 NIV

• •

When Martha asked Jesus to send her sister away from the disciples who were learning at His feet so that she could help prepare food for their guests, Jesus had to choose between the expectations of His culture and the gifts of Mary and Martha. Martha fully expected Jesus to take her side. Why else would she risk a public confrontation in front of their guests?

Surprisingly, the best thing for Martha wasn't necessarily what she wanted. While she wanted Jesus to remove Mary from an opportunity to learn with the disciples, she was actually trying to impose her gifts of hospitality on Mary. At the critical moment when Martha's frustration peaked, Jesus offered encouragement to both sisters, even if Martha received it as a rebuke. Jesus encouraged Mary to continue learning, to sit at His feet as a disciple, and to seek "what is better." At the same time, Jesus put Martha's many worries into perspective. She was concerned about a lot, but her gift of hospitality didn't have to leave her aggravated or resentful toward others. At a crucial moment, Jesus offered important insights that pointed both women toward fulfilling their callings.

Who do you know who needs encouragement to take risks or to find contentment and peace in their present circumstances? It could be someone in your own household.

God of heaven, we want to choose the better way and sit at the feet of our Savior, Jesus Christ. But so many things distract us— good things as well as selfish! Show us the balance so that we use our gifts but also honor You above all else.

Love That Breaks the Record Books

Love is patient, love is kind. It does not envy, it does not boast,
it is not proud. It does not dishonor others, it is not self-seeking,
it is not easily angered, it keeps no record of wrongs.
1 CORINTHIANS 13:4–5 NIV

• •

If we believe that God is love, as John assures us (1 John 4:8), and that love keeps no record of wrongs, then we have a staggering revelation on our hands. God's love isn't a conditional, record-keeping kind of love. Our wrongs have been forgiven *and* forgotten.

Perhaps our greatest barrier to loving others with this kind of generous abandon is our inability to receive God's love. We may believe that God can only love us if we pray more, live ashamed of our failures, or even hide our faults. This checklist approach to love alienates us from God and robs us of the experience of love that could revolutionize how we interact with our families, friends, and colleagues. Once we understand that God loves us and isn't keeping track of our wrongs, we'll begin to extend that generous love to others. That isn't to say others can't or won't hurt us. They will. But once we experience the depths of God's love and forgiveness for us, we'll have a solid foundation and assurance of our worth that doesn't require the approval of others.

When we know that we are loved without condition, we become free to extend the same forgiveness to others—a forgiveness that keeps no record of wrongs.

Perfect Father, You pursue us, and wait on us, and seek us at
every opportunity. You are the ideal parent, ready to forgive
and be reconciled whenever we go astray. Help us to accept
such a perfect love and to give You thanks for it every day.

Are We Passing Rules or the Story of God's Rule?

We will not hide them from their descendants;
we will tell the next generation the praiseworthy deeds
of the LORD, his power, and the wonders he has done.
PSALM 78:4 NIV

• •

It's easy to pass along rules and laws to younger generations and new believers, but the psalmist writes that rules aren't enough. While resolving to pass along the law of the Lord to the next generation, the writer of this psalm points us toward sharing the deeds of the Lord, His power, and the wonders He has done. This isn't just a matter of leading good Bible studies. The most powerful truth we can pass along is the power of God in our own lives. It's not enough to just pass along stories of God's power based on other people's stories—we have to live lives of faith and dependence that result in testimonies of God's presence and power. We need to demonstrate how the words of scripture have come to life in our daily lives, in our families, and in the workplace.

In fact, we are assured by Jesus that His followers will add to His testimony, and the early church in Acts repeatedly called themselves "witnesses" of God's deeds. If we haven't experienced the power and goodness of God for ourselves, what makes us think the next generation will do any better? If we hope to pass along the stories of God's power and deeds, we should first seek the presence of God so that our stories will be grounded in real-life experiences that we can relate to others.

O Lord, grant us a story worth passing on to our children! Give us a vision
and a passion for knowing You and sharing You that creates a bold life for
the world to see! Help us to face all temptation and conflict in the power
of Your Holy Spirit. Make us men who have something to pass on!

What Gets in the Way of God?

*Then Jesus said to his disciples, "Truly I tell you, it is hard
for someone who is rich to enter the kingdom of heaven.
Again I tell you, it is easier for a camel to go through the eye of a
needle than for someone who is rich to enter the kingdom of God."*
MATTHEW 19:23–24 NIV

• •

Jesus' words to the rich young ruler can be jarring, especially to readers in the western part of the world that tends to have more wealth. Perhaps we are joining the Philippian jailor in crying out, "What must I do to be saved?" According to Jesus, wealth is a tremendous obstacle to entering God's kingdom, and so those who want to remove any obstacle to God's kingdom need to ask some hard questions about their attachment to money and physical possessions.

Keep in mind that Jesus had wealthy followers. Jesus was supported by women with significant funds who cared for His needs. Wealth itself is not sinful. We all want to provide well for our families and be able to help others, too. Rather, wealth can become a substitute for God. The same goes for our possessions. We can rely on our possessions to provide comfort, to define our self-image, and to care for ourselves when we should be caring for the people around us. In other words, wealth can compete with treasuring God's kingdom over anything else.

The best way we can remove the obstacle of wealth is to practice regular generosity so that we learn to rely on God alone and minimize the distractions that could keep us from serving God and others.

God, You provide us with the ability to work and take care of our families. But we so easily feel the pull of money as a goal in itself! There always seems to be a new expense around every corner! Help us put our trust in Your faithfulness and to keep our hearts set on You.

How Do We Repent?

But Zacchaeus stood up and said to the Lord, "Look, Lord! Here and now I give half of my possessions to the poor, and if I have cheated anybody out of anything, I will pay back four times the amount."
LUKE 19:8 NIV

• •

We often hear pastors and teachers say that repentance means turning around and changing course. However, we may struggle to imagine what this could look like in our own lives. The story of Zacchaeus provides one of the most powerful pictures of true repentance in action. Zacchaeus didn't just commit to follow Jesus. He recognized that following Jesus meant he had to completely change his life according to the priorities and standards set by Jesus. He saw the invitation from Jesus as an opportunity to pursue a new course for his life. At his moment of conversion, Zacchaeus didn't just stop cheating people. He vowed to right the wrongs he had committed. He also pledged to give generously to the poor from his wealth. Zacchaeus recognized that much of his wealth had been acquired dishonestly, and he rightly recognized that following Jesus called for justice to those he'd wronged and the poor in his community whom he'd exploited as a tax collector for Rome. He signaled his newfound trust in Jesus and allegiance to the kingdom of God by removing the wealth and dishonest tactics that he had relied on for so long. Zacchaeus repented by not only changing his future, but by repairing his past.

Father, I want to experience true repentance. In You I am a new creation, and I will live my life according to Your will. But my past needs repair and redemption. I am confident You have forgiven me, so please show me how to right wrongs that I had a hand in. Give me Your eyes to see places that I can shine Your light and do good for Your glory.

We Are Directed by Our Delights

Blessed is the one who does not walk in step with the wicked or stand in the way that sinners take or sit in the company of mockers, but whose delight is in the law of the LORD, and who meditates on his law day and night. That person is like a tree planted by streams of water, which yields its fruit in season and whose leaf does not wither—whatever they do prospers.
PSALM 1:1–3 NIV

• •

We often speak of being delighted by events: a surprise visit with friends or family, receiving an unexpected windfall or promotion, being recognized publically or seeing our kids get an award at school. But we can also find delight in ongoing activities: sports, camping, cooking, coaching, etc. These ongoing sources of our delights can not only be enjoyed, but they can shed light on our spiritual health.

Our delights determine the direction of our lives. Perhaps we may be shocked to learn that God isn't interested in shutting down our delights or what gives us joy. Rather, God is interested in redirecting our delights and joys toward the most certain sources of both. In fact, these redirections aren't petty or frivolous. Although it may feel like a sacrifice at first, this is for our benefit. Those who follow the way of mockers and sinners will certainly find their own kinds of delights, but those delights will last only as long as the last punch line. Those who meditate on scripture and delight in communing with God will find a deeper, lasting delight that will carry them through the best and the worst that life has to offer. The delight offered by God takes time and commitment, but it's assured to last us.

Father, You created all things for us to enjoy—none more so than family. Help us to prayerfully consider all the things we give time and our hearts to and submit them continually to You. We want no delight, however good, to compete with Your proper place in our lives.

The Blessing of an Ending

Teach us to number our days, that we may gain a heart of wisdom.
PSALM 90:12 NIV

• •

Aging sparks no end of troubling moments and crisis points. There's a quarter-life crisis that hits around twenty-five, the mid-life crisis at forty, and then a crisis that typically hits around the sixties as many look into retirement. Sometimes, if we lose our focus on Christ during the crisis, we may find less wisdom and more regret and recklessness as yet another year passes by.

Each crisis of aging is rooted in the realization that death comes for us all and that our time on this earth is limited. However, the writer of this psalm assures us that numbering our days with the end in mind can actually lead us to greater peace and wisdom. Perhaps this strikes some as impossible, but consider this—once we view our days as limited, aren't we compelled to consider how to use them best? Doesn't each day become all the more valuable once we see that our days aren't available in an endless supply?

The wisdom that the psalmist talks about will help us ask hard questions about how we spend our time. We may be more driven to prioritize time spent in prayer. We may set aside more time to invest in our children's lives. We may change our professional goals or at least measure our success by different means. As we number our days with an awareness of their limited supply, we will have greater clarity when discerning our priorities and will find greater peace in the knowledge of God's presence throughout each day.

God of endless days, You have granted us a small amount of time to live by faith and not by sight. Help us spend our time so that we are happy to see You when the day comes, and wise about the investments we make for Your kingdom.

Hope for Doubters

He said to them, "How foolish you are, and how slow to believe
all that the prophets have spoken! Did not the Messiah have
to suffer these things and then enter his glory?" And beginning
with Moses and all the Prophets, he explained to them what
was said in all the Scriptures concerning himself.
LUKE 24:25–27 NIV

• •

At one point or another in our lives, we all struggle through situations that test our faith or cause us to question the goodness of God. Perhaps we can't make sense of the profound loss of a child or the collapse of our marriage, or our faith just wears down gradually as one hard season gives way to another. It's in the hard times that no one questions Jesus' declaration, "In this world you will have trouble."

In the story of the disciples along the road to Emmaus, we find two disciples of Jesus who have essentially given up. They're confused and fearful, and they've most certainly left Jerusalem for fear of losing their lives. As far as we can tell, they believe Jesus' movement is finished. If they expected Jesus to rise from the dead, they would have stayed around. Despite their doubts and, as Jesus said, foolishness, Jesus still showed up, explaining the scriptures to them and eventually revealing Himself in the breaking of bread.

While it's true that doubt and unbelief can undermine our ability to follow Jesus, this story reminds us that Jesus won't discard His followers who struggle or who pass through a season of doubts. Whether we're looking for Him or just walking along in confusion, all is not lost. He is more than willing to show up and lead us back to faith.

LORD, my God, You will not—cannot—leave me alone
in my darkest times! Open my eyes, Lord, to see You!

Our Daily Bread vs. Our Eternal Bread

"Do not work for food that spoils, but for food that endures to eternal life, which the Son of Man will give you. For on him God the Father has placed his seal of approval."
JOHN 6:27 NIV

• •

When Jesus taught His disciples how to pray, He told them to ask God for the provision of their daily bread. Daily bread isn't something that you can store up for the long term, especially back in Jesus' day. He didn't instruct them to pray for storehouses of grain or even reserves of coins that would give them the ability to manage any crisis. They were welcome to ask God for provision, but only daily provision.

How often are we tempted to pray for a long-term solution to our problems and needs? It's almost maddening to think that a God with limitless resources would instruct us to ask for so small a provision, but then perhaps Jesus knew something of human ambition and our tendency to rely on our possessions and resources rather than God. Ironically, even our best "long-term" solutions are actually quite limited and fleeting.

The presence of Christ in our lives and a long-term faith in Him will never let us down, but our strength, finances, and even relationships may well let us down when we need them the most. The only sure long-term bet is the eternal bread of Jesus Himself present in our lives, nourishing us and providing for our needs day by day.

Feed me today, Father, with Your Word! Help me to throw my cares on You because You care for me! How little I trust in You sometimes— when You are the very source of all life and purpose. Help me to stop scraping by spiritually and to feast on the Bread of Life!

God Treats Us as We'd Treat Ourselves

"If you, then, though you are evil, know how to give good gifts to your children, how much more will your Father in heaven give good gifts to those who ask him! So in everything, do to others what you would have them do to you, for this sums up the Law and the Prophets."
MATTHEW 7:11–12 NIV

• •

At a time when the religious believed that following God required adhering to a long list of laws and avoiding particular people, Jesus cut through the expectations of His audience with a very simple summary of the Law and Prophets. "Caring for others as we would care for ourselves" forced His audience to stop placing barriers between each other and to treat each other with mercy.

However, Jesus isn't just talking about the way we treat each other in this passage. His focus is much wider than personal interactions. He assured His listeners that God is far more kind and merciful than anticipated. We shouldn't be surprised to find an assurance of God's goodness followed by a command to be kind and merciful to each other. Jesus is asking us to imitate God's mercy and generosity that we've received. Just as God mercifully gives good gifts the way a father would to his own children, we should extend the same kindness to each other.

Generous Father, You are the Giver of all good things! As human fathers, we can begin to see Your heart in dealing with us, though Your love and mercy are beyond compare. Help us to treat others with the same care and concern we would want for ourselves, and in doing so, please You.

What Does It Mean to Live by Faith?

*Who may ascend the mountain of the LORD? Who may stand in
his holy place? The one who has clean hands and a pure heart,
who does not trust in an idol or swear by a false god.*
PSALM 24:3–4 NIV

. . . .

Living by faith each day requires more than believing in the saving work
of Christ on the cross. That's just the starting point for our life in Christ!
Just as having a child is the beginning of a living relationship, so is the
life of faith. It's manifested in our day-to-day decisions when we have
to choose whether or not we will trust God to care and provide for us.

When the writer of this psalm says that those who stand in God's holy
place will not trust in an idol or swear by a false god, we would do well to
remember that idols and false gods weren't just passing fads or sources
of personal fulfillment in Old Testament times. Idols and false gods were
trusted to provide essentials for life, such as rain for crops or fertility for
future children. Some Israelites surely felt tempted to mix prayers to the
Lord with prayers to an idol in order to cover all of their bases.

Those who live by faith in God place their trust in God alone for their
daily needs, believing that their obedience will not be in vain. The kind of
faith God requires means placing all of our hope in God's provision and
deliverance rather than wealth, our personal influence, or relationships
with people in power.

*I praise You, Father of Life, for bringing me to life in Christ Jesus
and introducing me to a living relationship with You! You are my goal,
my source, my strength, my endurance in all things. Help me to live
a life of faith through the Holy Spirit in all my daily needs.*

Will Jesus Restore Us after Failure?

The third time he said to him, "Simon son of John, do you love me?" Peter was hurt because Jesus asked him the third time, "Do you love me?" He said, "Lord, you know all things; you know that I love you." Jesus said, "Feed my sheep."
JOHN 21:17 NIV

. . . .

Every dad experiences the failures of his kids as they learn right from wrong. It's part of the job and, even more, part of a father's nature. We don't disown our kids for their sins and weaknesses. But sometimes we don't give God as much credit. Sometimes we imagine that Jesus can't do much of anything with us after we've failed. Maybe we believe we've been disqualified or have fallen away because of our misconduct. Maybe we believe that grace only works up to a point, and we've gone too far beyond it. Peter committed the grave sin of denying Jesus, though he had been with Him daily for three years and had witnessed and experienced miracle after miracle. Still Peter essentially chose to cut himself off from Jesus when his life could have been on the line.

How did Jesus respond to Peter? First, Jesus went to the heart of the matter: "Do you love me?" Despite Peter's failure, Jesus still offered mercy to Peter because He recognized that Peter still loved Him, even if that love was imperfect and prone to fail at times. Second, Jesus restored Peter immediately, tasking him with caring for His followers. While we can hardly use this as a catchall template for all sins, Jesus was quick to turn Peter from a denier to an affirmer. The point person in teaching others about Jesus was the man who had denied Him. Peter's love for Jesus made the difference when his future hung in the balance, and Jesus restored him even after the most humbling of failures.

God of restoration, we thank You for Your great patience and love! How wonderful are Your ways, and beyond understanding! Thank You for pursuing us!

Why We Should Put Others First

Do nothing out of selfish ambition or vain conceit. Rather,
in humility value others above yourselves, not looking to your
own interests but each of you to the interests of the others.
PHILIPPIANS 2:3–4 NIV

• •

No kid in the world ever started out sharing his toys—it was something he had to be taught. Most of the conflict we face in life is rooted in seeking our own interests above those of others. Our ambitions to succeed can be a healthy expression of our talents and gifts, but they can also put us at odds with others if our success becomes linked to prospering at the expense of others.

When we place our needs ahead of others, we're bound for conflict, as plenty of other people will also seek their own needs first and foremost. Paul's solution to conflict is stepping back and seeking out the interests of others above our own. Beyond removing potential points of conflict from our lives, this also forces us to trust God in the same way that Christ trusted God with His life on earth. Rather than seeking our own exaltation at the expense of others, we can trust that God will see and reward our selflessness and generosity.

Jesus assured us that the first will be last and the last will be first. We can save ourselves from a lot of anger and conflict by choosing to be last, putting the needs of others first, and making ourselves a servant above all else. While we can strive to use our gifts well, servants never seek their own benefit at the expense of others.

Father, help me to see where I am seeking my own interests at the expense of others and to offer myself as a servant of Your kingdom first. Help me to be humble and put the needs of others above my own, knowing that You will be my Provider and my Sustainer.

Love Begins with Faith

We love because he first loved us. Whoever claims to love
God yet hates a brother or sister is a liar. For whoever does not
love their brother and sister, whom they have seen, cannot love
God, whom they have not seen. And he has given us this command:
Anyone who loves God must also love their brother and sister.

1 JOHN 4:19–21 NIV

• •

If we live in fear of God's judgment or condemnation, there's a good chance we'll let that fear define how we treat others. Our image of God will determine how we treat others. Jesus assured us that those who have received mercy will extend the same mercy to others. When John writes about love, it's from the perspective of someone who sees God's love with tremendous clarity. His worth is determined according to God's love for him. Out of that deep reserve of love and acceptance, John found that he was able to extend that love to others. In fact, the best way to gauge our relationship with God is how we treat others.

If we are able to love others, then we have experienced the love and acceptance of God. If we are fearful, angry, or uncaring toward others, then we are most likely living out of fear, defensiveness, or judgment. The clearest indicator is in our own households. How do we treat those most dear to us? How do we respond to our kids when they disobey? How quickly do we forgive and show mercy and unconditional love? Our families know the answer to these questions—they experience it every day. Do we?

Showing love may require some effort on our part, but it most certainly begins with faith: believing that God loves us. That foundation of love makes it possible to love and accept others regardless of how they have treated us.

Father of love, help me to know You more fully so that my actions
will be consistent with what You would want out of a faithful son.

Does God Have Your Attention?

Do not be like the horse or the mule, which have no understanding
but must be controlled by bit and bridle or they will not come to
you. Many are the woes of the wicked, but the LORD's unfailing
love surrounds the one who trusts in him.
PSALM 32:9–10 NIV

• •

C. S. Lewis wrote, "God whispers to us in our pleasures, speaks in our conscience, but shouts in our pains: it is his megaphone to rouse a deaf world." Many can relate to this, as God often seems most present when we are suffering personally or struggling with the suffering of another—a sick child or spouse, an aging parent.

So often a difficult situation prompts us to rely on God in new ways. The writer of this psalm suggests that those who fail to trust in God must be led like a horse, and sometimes our pain and difficult situations can feel like a bit or bridle that drags us back to God. The solution, according to this psalm, is to understand and to trust God's unfailing love to surround us whether our lives are difficult or pleasant. In fact, those who trust in God's unfailing love will be spared the many struggles and disappointments that the wicked face. It's a lesson we long to see our children embrace, but sometimes we miss it ourselves.

While the trusting and untrusting will pass through difficult seasons of life, the difference will be that God's loving presence will carry us through our pain. God's gentle love moves around us. It doesn't drag us or force us to act in a particular way. It is a love that is present and comforting, remaining faithful even when we wander and become stubborn yet again.

Good Father, forgive me when I've made You drag me along
like a mule instead of walking with You like a son! Help me
to lean on You fully in all my thinking and in all my choices—
to draw near to You and enjoy Your company.

Suffering Makes Us Confident

The Spirit himself testifies with our spirit that we are
God's children. Now if we are children, then we are heirs—
heirs of God and co-heirs with Christ, if indeed we share in
his sufferings in order that we may also share in his glory.
ROMANS 8:16–17 NIV

• •

Perhaps our first thought in a season of suffering or persecution is that something is terribly wrong. If we are God's children, shouldn't life get easier? We will no doubt pray that our suffering ends soon and that God will bring us relief. However, Paul encourages us to think of suffering in far different terms.

Besides the comforting testimony of the Holy Spirit that we are God's children because we suffer, we also can look to our suffering as an act of solidarity with the sufferings of Christ.

If we suffer because of our allegiance to Christ, we'll place ourselves firmly among God's children who can look forward to sharing in glory one day. While we shouldn't hope for our suffering to continue indefinitely, God may give us our greatest confidence and hope of future glory in the midst of our darkest moments today. Jesus assured us that His own sufferings signaled that the same would surely come to His followers one day.

If you're going through a season of suffering or isolation because of your faith, that doesn't mean God has abandoned you. Rather, it means that this world has recognized you belong to a different family and your hope is in a different place.

Father, any suffering You allow is a blessing. Hard as it may be to
endure, You are offering us the chance to stand beside Your Son and
be His brother. You have made us heirs in Christ—help us to be faithful
sons, as Jesus was, when we are asked to endure the things He did.

Receiving God's Gift like a Child

But Jesus called the children to him and said, "Let the little children come to me, and do not hinder them, for the kingdom of God belongs to such as these. Truly I tell you, anyone who will not receive the kingdom of God like a little child will never enter it."
LUKE 18:16–17 NIV

. . . .

We can all recall what it's like to give a gift to a child. She may well cling to it for hours if we let her. Some children may even obsess over keeping the box that the gift came in, re-creating the moment they opened it over and over again.

Children offer their complete attention to gifts, receiving them with joy and focus. There is a simplicity and lack of cynicism among children that allows them to be fully present in the moment. They are brimming over with faith, hope, and joy rather than doubts, fears, and arguments. Perhaps Jesus had grown weary of the latter when He embraced a group of children despite His disciples' efforts to keep them away. Their eagerness to learn and to receive His blessing offers the perfect picture for receiving God's kingdom. For a kingdom that is compared to a tiny seed or little flecks of yeast that are worked through the bread, children are the most likely to perceive its value. Rather than coming up with sophisticated explanations for or against Jesus, they demonstrated that coming to Jesus with open arms is the perfect place to begin.

Father, how quickly we forget the simple lessons we learned as children. You are delighted by the uncomplicated faith kids have! Help us to unwind our thoughts and feelings and return to the genuine faith and enthusiasm of a child! Thank You, Father.

Bold like Dad

*According to his eternal purpose that he accomplished in
Christ Jesus our Lord. In him and through faith in him
we may approach God with freedom and confidence.*
EPHESIANS 3:11–12 NIV

• •

God wants His children to share in His personality, to take on His likeness, to live like Him. Boldness is often one of the overlooked traits that He wants us to experience. God is bold, invading history, overturning kingdoms, interrupting our well-crafted plans to have a relationship with us; and by doing so, He risks the very opposite—our rejection. His great boldness can only come from His great love. He has not withheld even His own Son (Romans 8:2–3) to bring us into a life-giving relationship with Himself. Writer Francis Chan has coined a name for this kind of relentless pursuit—"Crazy Love." It's the kind of love that makes no excuses for its audacity.

So what does a bold, seeking Father enjoy seeing in His offspring? Reluctance? Hesitance? Or the kind of boldness He Himself demonstrated toward us? What would please Him more than having His children throwing off everything that hinders them (Hebrews 12:1) and approaching Him with freedom and confidence (Ephesians 3:12), knowing He made it possible? In Christ, our boldness pleases the Father, because it tells Him that we are His. Boldness isn't disrespectful as long as we know who made it possible for us to enjoy it. Rather, we are bearing His likeness, showing ourselves to be His children.

If we are to reflect His image, then we must strike out and approach Him with freedom and confidence, just the way Dad likes it.

*Father, make me bold like You! Let me love without
fear and bear the burdens of others with grace.
Teach me to enjoy being Your fearless son!*

A Fool's Game

"The king reflected and said, 'Is this not Babylon the great, which I myself have built as a royal residence by the might of my power and for the glory of my majesty?' While the word was in the king's mouth, a voice came from heaven, saying, 'King Nebuchadnezzar, to you it is declared: sovereignty has been removed from you, and you will be driven away from mankind, and your dwelling place will be with the beasts of the field. . .until you recognize that the Most High is ruler over the realm of mankind and bestows it on whomever He wishes.' "

DANIEL 4:30–32 NASB

• •

Success and achievement are great—unless they lead you to forget basic spiritual truths. Truths like "You cannot really accomplish anything apart from God." He is the *Most High,* and no matter how much we may achieve on earth, our "success" is ultimately His gift, for His purposes.

Another spiritual truth that's easily forgotten in the midst of success is that arrogance always invites correction. As the apostle Peter says, "God is opposed to the proud, but gives grace to the humble" (1 Peter 5:5 NASB). He doesn't ignore the proud or work around them—He actively opposes them. When we are tempted to slap ourselves on the back, we should take note, as Nebuchadnezzar eventually did, that we are playing a fool's game. And you don't have to be some prideful overachiever to get God's attention. Anyone who takes credit for what God has done can enjoy His harsh mercy. God rebukes the foolishness of high and low alike, because He is merciful to all.

Father of all good things, remind us where our successes come from. If our work is blessed, it is from You; if our marriage is strong, it is Your gift; if our children grow to be honorable, we have only You to thank. Apart from You we can do nothing.

Opening Your Eyes

For since the creation of the world His invisible attributes, His eternal
power and divine nature, have been clearly seen, being understood
through what has been made, so that they are without excuse.
ROMANS 1:20 NASB

• •

Invisibility doesn't mean inaccessibility. Just because a thing cannot be seen doesn't mean it can't be known or understood in some meaningful way. The air we breathe is an example. So are the inner qualities of people: diligence, intelligence, impatience; the love our children feel before they can walk or talk. When we see a beautiful painting, we see clearly the invisible quality called *talent*. In the same way, God declares that at least two of His invisible qualities have been "clearly seen" from the creation itself. First, His eternal power, that He is outside of time, without beginning and without end. We don't have to wonder who came before Him or who will come after Him. What He promises to mankind will endure since there are no circumstances that can surprise Him. The second invisible quality is His divine nature. He is above the created order and not one of us. He was not born and will not die. He is the first and final authority of all things.

The irony of seeing the invisible is resolved in creation itself. The fullest revelation of God in Christ is not required for God to hold mankind accountable for at least the two qualities He has published across time and space. As the psalmist writes: "The heavens are telling of the glory of God; and their expanse is declaring the work of His hands. Day to day pours forth speech, and night to night reveals knowledge" (Psalm 19:1–2 NASB).

Gracious Father, You have made Yourself known through all of creation
from the beginning of time. And You have left a witness in our hearts
to Your presence from our earliest days. Help us to see You in all things
and to share with our families the ability to see the invisible.

Overflowing

*For we wanted to come to you—I, Paul, more than once—
and yet Satan hindered us. For who is our hope or joy or
crown of exultation? Is it not even you, in the presence of
our Lord Jesus at His coming? For you are our glory and joy.*
1 THESSALONIANS 2:18–20 NASB

. . . .

Paul's enthusiasm for the Thessalonian believers bursts forth in these words, using language usually reserved for God Himself. Imagine! Paul's "hope" and "joy" and "glory" are tied to this small group of people into whom he has poured his life. When Jesus returns, Paul plans on showing them off.

When we come to Christ, we begin our experience as a child of God. We are adopted (Romans 8:15) and begin rethinking our lives as one of His offspring. Then as we share our faith and help people grow in Christ, we begin to see the *other* side of the relationship—the parental side. God's side. This is what Paul is expressing, and why he speaks so joyfully. He's displaying the same excited attitude toward the Thessalonians that God has about all of us—pride and joy!

Paul reflects God's joy toward his own "children" in the faith because God's parental joy is contagious. Like Paul did with the Thessalonians, God rejoices over us, brags about us, dotes on us, and takes pride in us—and the things He's preparing in heaven for those who love Him are beyond imagination (1 Corinthians 2:9). When we see Him face-to-face, we will truly understand what an extravagant parent God is. We will rejoice in Him, and He will rejoice in us.

*Good Father, I am humbled by Your affection! I know what it is
to rejoice over my own children, but somehow it's hard to believe
You feel that way toward me. Help me to see myself as You do
and enjoy my place as Your beloved son in Christ.*

The Living and Working Word

*We also constantly thank God that when you received the word
of God which you heard from us, you accepted it not as the
word of men, but for what it really is, the word of God,
which also performs its work in you who believe.*

1 THESSALONIANS 2:13 NASB

• •

In the first chapter of the Bible, we see that God's spoken Word was powerful enough to bring all of creation into being. John 1 further explains that the "Word of God" is the person of Jesus Christ Himself, through whom all things were created and find their purpose. Throughout the Bible, we see that God's Word continues to work since the beginning—giving life, protecting, enlightening, redeeming, effecting change according to God's will. " 'So will My word be which goes forth from My mouth; it will not return to Me empty, without accomplishing what I desire, and without succeeding in the matter for which I sent it' " (Isaiah 55:11 NASB).

God's Word works because it is alive. Jesus, the Word Himself, declares that "the words that I have spoken to you are spirit and are life" (John 6:63 NASB). Like a six-year-old kid, the Word of God simply can't sit still!

Paul was delighted with the Thessalonians because they accepted his message as the authoritative, purposeful, and living thing that it was and, by doing so, opened up its divine power to work in their lives.

*Word of Life, You created all things, and You hold all things together.
The words You spoke from the beginning, You are still speaking today.
Work in our lives and the lives of our families to hear and to respond.*

Down to the Top

The LORD came down on Mount Sinai, to the top of the mountain;
and the LORD called Moses to the top of the mountain, and Moses went up.
EXODUS 19:20 NASB

• •

Moses received the Law from God in a dramatic face-to-face meeting. And He chose an unusual place to do it considering Moses was about eighty years old—the top of a mountain. God had Moses make the arduous climb to the top of Mount Sinai alone to meet with Him. A truly remarkable feat at his age—it was no doubt painful and exhausting, requiring perseverance and commitment. But even at the top of a mountain, there was yet a distance between Moses and God. Even if Moses had ascended the highest peak on earth, God would still have had to close the gap by coming *down* to meet with him. And this is *Moses*—a central figure in Israel's history—who was called by God at the burning bush, who faced Pharaoh and the power of Egypt, who parted the Red Sea! And even Moses could not completely close the distance between man and God.

In this story lives a beautiful metaphor of man's need to have God fill the space that always remains even after we have done everything we can do to reach Him. No amount of human effort will ever connect us to God—we are the children that must be picked up by their Father to see Him face-to-face.

How wonderful that we do not have to have Moses' résumé or repeat his grueling trip up a mountain; we have perfect access to God through Christ who forever closes the gap.

Father, You reach down to me in my sin and powerlessness
to bring me to Yourself. You, and You alone, have brought
this about, and it is marvelous to behold. I am so grateful
to be Your son through Jesus, my Savior!

The Odds Are in Your Favor

The Spirit of the Lord GOD is upon me, because the LORD has anointed me to bring good news to the afflicted; He has sent me to bind up the brokenhearted, to proclaim liberty to captives, and freedom to prisoners; to proclaim the favorable year of the LORD, and the day of vengeance of our God.
ISAIAH 61:1–2 NASB

• •

Our God is an amazingly giving Person. He sent His Son to bring the good news of a truly amazing opportunity. Christ was sent to proclaim "the favorable year of the Lord" and "the day" of judgment by God. That's a 365 to 1 ratio in our favor! This propitious arrangement is symbolic of God's great mercy and patience, "not wishing for any to perish but for all to come to repentance" (2 Peter 3:9 NASB). As fathers we see a glimpse of His patience when we yearn for our children to turn from their errors and enjoy the life we know they were called to.

Sometimes God's forbearance goes beyond what make sense to us. Even Jesus' disciples didn't quickly grasp this divine patience, eager to "command fire to come down from heaven and consume" those who rejected Christ (Luke 9:54 NASB). The Lord's response was firm: "But He turned and rebuked them, and said, 'You do not know what kind of spirit you are of; for the Son of Man did not come to destroy men's lives, but to save them'" (Luke 9:55–56 NASB).

God wants all to repent. To confuse this time of favor and opportunity is to be of a different spirit than the Lord; not "regard[ing] the patience of our Lord as salvation" (2 Peter 3:15 NASB) is to miss God's heart and the chance to be part of it.

Patient Father, I am grateful for Your willingness to endure all things for the sake of my repentance. Please help me to be of that same Spirit, starting with my own family.

Not So Fast

Now when He was in Jerusalem at the Passover, during the feast,
many believed in His name, observing His signs which He was doing.
But Jesus, on His part, was not entrusting Himself to them, for He
knew all men, and because He did not need anyone to testify
concerning man, for He Himself knew what was in man.
JOHN 2:23–25 NASB

• •

We all know from experience how different we can be from one day to the next. Everything from the temperature of the room to our greatest fear can change our moods and influence our decisions—our families can testify to this!

As history shows, our unstable nature makes certain things inevitable: conflict, political unrest, war. As an old saying goes, *the only thing constant in life is change.* Not that change is bad in itself. On the contrary, we would never see revival if change couldn't also be positive. But the very fact that we are creatures prone to extremes means we must be watched closely. Jesus knew this better than anyone. Even though He went through changes while on earth from birth to resurrection, He was stable in His essential nature and purpose—unlike those who surrounded Him. Fickle crowds would follow Him one day awed by His miracles and teachings, and the next try to throw Him off a cliff (Luke 4:29)! The crowd that sang "Hosanna" as He rode into Jerusalem would be the same crowd that days later cried, "Crucify Him!" This is why Jesus would not be swayed by popularity. He looked beyond earthly success to His eternal Father whom He could trust as the only true unchanging Source.

Unchanging Father, You alone are my source of identity and purpose.
Help me to become the same man day after day, not giving in to
every wind that blows but keeping in step with Your Holy Spirit.

The Divine Promise

*God made great and marvelous promises, so that his nature
would become part of us. Then we could escape our evil
desires and the corrupt influences of this world.*
2 PETER 1:4 CEV

• •

Simply avoiding hell isn't the point of salvation. Arguably that might be enough from a human perspective, but God has something more in mind for us, something far more interesting and exciting.

God's plan, as incredible as it may sound, is that we should partake in, and reflect, His own divine nature. He wants children that look and sound and act like their Father, free from corruption inside and out. "Therefore, having these promises, beloved, let us cleanse ourselves from all defilement of flesh and spirit, perfecting holiness in the fear of God" (2 Corinthians 7:1 NASB).

What were God's promises? That He would live among His people and be their God, that they would be set apart from the world, even counted as His sons and daughters (2 Corinthians 6). How are those promises fulfilled? Through His Holy Spirit living in us: "When you believed, you were marked in him with a seal, the promised Holy Spirit" (Ephesians 1:13 NIV).

The role of the Holy Spirit is to create a people who could freely and honestly interact with the Father—the way any father would want his children to act—but without His working in us, nothing in our experience will ever change and He won't get the children He wants. Only through the Holy Spirit indwelling and empowering us can we live out the full plan of our salvation.

*What an honor, to be given Your very nature!
We praise You for Your great and precious gift!*

The Flip Side of Faith

*But My righteous one shall live by faith; and if he
shrinks back, My soul has no pleasure in him.*
HEBREWS 10:38 NASB

• •

People usually assume that doubt is the opposite of faith. But in the New Testament (NASB) the words *doubt* or *doubting* appear only a handful of times, while *fear* or *afraid* show up over one hundred times. The life of faith is more often a battle against fear than doubt, the way a child learns to trust his father during a swimming lesson.

Fear certainly was the synagogue official's test when, in faith, he had begged for Jesus to heal his sick daughter. Then his little girl died. Jesus, knowing the man's heart, comforted him with these words, "Do not be afraid any longer, only believe" (Mark 5:36 NASB).

Later, Jesus, knowing the fear Peter would face after He was arrested, said, "Simon, Simon, behold, Satan has demanded permission to sift you like wheat; but I have prayed for you, that your faith may not fail" (Luke 22:31–32 NASB).

Of course God is not pleased when His people give in to fear, because it means we are shrinking back from Him. But the good news is that we have a Father and a Savior who knows our weakness and "has not given us a spirit of timidity, but of power and love and discipline" (2 Timothy 1:7 NASB). We move forward in faith as we keep in step with the Spirit who is our Helper (John 14:16). We may well wrestle with fear, but we are never alone in the struggle.

*Father, just as I don't want my children to pull back from me in fear,
You are not pleased when we give in to fears that interrupt our
relationship. I want to move toward You every day in some way, large or
small. Help me to become more like Your Son, who always trusted You.*

A Good Foundation

See to it that no one takes you captive through philosophy and empty deception, according to the tradition of men, according to the elementary principles of the world, rather than according to Christ.
Colossians 2:8 nasb

• •

The test of every building is in its foundation. No matter how fine in appearance it is, if the foundation is faulty, the whole structure is at risk. Sadly, this is also the way our lives can be if we build our thinking on faulty reasoning and shifting philosophies.

The world offers its perspective and solutions to our problems twenty-four hours a day, over television and radio, in bookstores and newspapers, and around the lunch table. The voice of this world rarely lacks confidence, and the advice often seems wise and time tested. The proponents of worldly philosophies may even mean well, but they don't perceive the empty nature of their own beliefs. Why would they? *If it was good enough for Dad*, it's reasoned, *it's good enough for me.* Traditions passed down from one generation to the next carry weight whether they're right or wrong.

Then there are those current worldviews specifically designed for the marketplace—money-making offerings pushed in books, DVDs, and infomercials. They are easily identified because they are built on the simplest principles of this world: promotion of self, pursuit of pleasure, get-rich-quick schemes, emphasis on appearance, promises of simple solutions to complex problems.

But Christ offers truth, reality, and a future that is eternal, rather than fleeting. If we build upon His work and His words, we will avoid the captivity of a dying world and the loss of our opportunity for a solid foundation.

God, our Father, thank You for Your Word
and a way to understand how to live in freedom.

Just Don't

The LORD God commanded the man, saying, "From any
tree of the garden you may eat freely; but from the tree
of the knowledge of good and evil you shall not eat,
for in the day that you eat from it you will surely die."
GENESIS 2:16–17 NASB

• •

Adam and Eve were designed to enjoy uninterrupted union with God, and the only "don't" for them was eating the fruit that would end that joy. But of course they went directly against that single commandment, passing on that tendency to their children and all generations that followed. Their one act of disobedience multiplied into all the things we call sin today. No wonder the "don'ts" seem to multiply throughout the Bible. . .they're just keeping pace with the ways man has invented to disregard God.

Some people dismiss the Bible as a mere collection of rules and restrictions. This misses the original purpose of God to have "a people for His own possession out of all the peoples who are on the face of the earth" (Deuteronomy 7:6 NASB). The Old Testament Law was a gift to set His people apart and increase their joy, not end it. It was ultimately designed to lead people to Christ (Galatians 3:24), people who would fulfill God's original purpose when He "gave Himself for us to redeem us from every lawless deed, and to purify for Himself a people for His own possession" (Titus 2:14 NASB). Now the things we consider "don'ts" from God do not constitute a law—they provide real freedom and create a holy experience with our Lord. Any "don't" from Him equates to life for us.

Father, You have given us the path to a life of peace by saying "do not"
to many things—things that would destroy us! Thank You for Your
loving limits in our lives, though we don't always appreciate them
any more than our children understand why we limit them!

Sorry I Asked

Then the LORD answered Job out of the storm and said, "Now gird up your loins like a man; I will ask you, and you instruct Me. Will you really annul My judgment? Will you condemn Me that you may be justified?"
JOB 40:6–8 NASB

• •

Sometimes people lament that God doesn't answer them in their suffering. They look at Job and think, *At least God answered Job.* True, but look at the answer! God *rebukes* Job, confronting him with a harshness that seems inappropriate considering his painful circumstances. But God's had enough of being questioned; now it's Job's turn.

Chapter after chapter, Job has complained that he's done nothing to deserve his situation, and he was right. God Himself declared Job "blameless" and "upright" in Job 1:8. Yet Job's friends argued that his suffering was the consequence of sin, though Job knew better. They were rebuked because they condemned him without being able to address his argument. Job's rebuke was different. His error wasn't some hidden sin, or even a faulty argument, but in forgetting whom he was addressing. He was demanding that God justify Himself, explain Himself, even defend Himself.

"Oh, if only someone would give me a hearing! I've signed my name to my defense—let the Almighty One answer! I want to see my indictment in writing" (Job 31:35–6 MSG).

Job would have the "Almighty One" stand beside him in front of another judge and make His case. Job would see God condemned to justify his own understanding.

When we suffer, let us "pour out [our] complaint" to God (Psalm 142:2 NASB) as a Father who wants His children to lean on Him, but always remembering whom we are talking to!

You, O God, are not to be taken lightly! We humble ourselves rather than demand answers; we wait for You rather than accuse; we hope in You rather than choose our own path.

Freedom's Purpose

All things are lawful for me, but not all things are profitable.
All things are lawful for me, but I will not be mastered by anything.
1 CORINTHIANS 6:12 NASB

• •

Grace wouldn't be grace if it didn't allow us room to make mistakes without fear of losing our relationship with God. Grace is God's determination that our sin will not stand between Him and us. As believers we have come to accept Christ's work alone for our reconciliation to God. In Christ, God fulfills the demands that the Old Testament Law made upon man and eliminates our need to rely on any set of laws to make us acceptable to Him.

But there is always the chance that such a wonderful freedom can be misused. As writer Philip Yancey says, "Grace implies a risk, the risk that we might abuse it." Sort of like giving your son a bike to ride to school—he can also use that bike to skip it!

Some Corinthian believers, freed from the arduous burden of legalism, were using their new "freedom" as an excuse to indulge in unprofitable things—a spiritual waste of time. Some had gone further, becoming addicted to activities that, although technically allowable, had replaced God as the focus of their lives. How absurd to think that God's gift of grace would push aside the One who gave it! The whole point of grace was to free us to move *toward* our Father, not away.

No amount of rationalizing should overrule godly common sense (Hebrews 5:14). God wants preeminence in our lives, and even death will be overcome to achieve this end. So for today, let us use our freedom to become like Him, not test the limits of His patience.

God of freedom, You have a very specific idea of what
freedom is—and many times we miss the point! Open our
eyes to the wisdom of using our freedom to draw closer
to You, rather than waste our time and test Your patience!

Always the Best Policy

Truthful lips will be established forever,
but a lying tongue is only for a moment.
PROVERBS 12:19 NASB

• •

If you've ever looked your child in the eye and wondered if they were telling you the truth, then you understand the uneasy feeling it creates. Sometimes, of course, it's easy to tell when a person is lying, like when your kid blurts out, "It wasn't me!"

Even if people don't outright lie to you but just "shade the truth," is that any less deceptive? Maybe the consequences are less severe for a child with cookie crumbs on his mouth than a man with blood on his hands, but neither is without deceit. The acorn of deception may not always grow into an oak, but it still has all the same DNA—whether we plan the lie or whether it just pops out when we're caught off guard.

The value God places on truthfulness has always been made plain in the Bible. The power of truth is that it lasts. It's eternal because it comes from the very nature of God. Jesus claimed to be "the truth" itself (John 14:6 NASB) and promised that "the truth will make you free" (John 8:32 NASB). God wants us to live in truth and the Truth to live in us. "Behold, You desire truth in the innermost being" (Psalm 51:6 NASB), and so God sends the Helper who is "the Spirit of truth" (John 15:26 NASB) to indwell believers. We keep pace with the Holy Spirit by living honestly and affirm our connection to God as His children. Truth is our heritage and our birthright as members of God's family.

Father of truth, You can't do anything but be honest! Deception of any
kind is not in Your nature, nor does it honor You in Your children.
Help me to live an honest life, without fear of the consequences of truth.

Who Is God's Will?

*"I searched for a man among them who would build
up the wall and stand in the gap before Me for the land,
so that I would not destroy it; but I found no one."*
EZEKIEL 22:30 NASB

. . . .

When God wanted to do something on the earth to make Himself known or to teach His people, He always started with a person. Think of the history of the Bible—it's the story of people who demonstrated faith. Prophets, kings, parents, soldiers, builders, fishermen—these are some of the *who* of God's will—men and women who became the fulcrum for God to move the world.

God's approach to working His will among mankind hasn't changed. God is still looking for individuals who will stand with Him and answer the call the way Isaiah did: "Then I heard the voice of the Lord, saying, 'Whom shall I send, and who will go for Us?' Then I said, 'Here am I. Send me!'" (Isaiah 6:8 NASB).

Of course, the ultimate *who* in God's will is His Son, Jesus of Nazareth—"All things have been created through him and for him. He is before all things, and in him all things hold together" (Colossians 1:16–17 NIV). And He came "to purify for Himself a people for His own possession, zealous for good deeds" (Titus 2:14 NASB). Through Christ, we have the privilege of becoming the *who* God is seeking to "build up the wall and stand in the gap."

Father, You work through us despite our imperfections. You seek people who will give themselves to You without reserve. Help us to become that person and to raise that kind of person up from our own household.

The Greatest Teacher

"Behold, God is exalted in His power; who is a teacher like Him?"
JOB 36:22 NASB

• •

God is a gracious and faithful Teacher, and this life is His classroom. Lessons begin with the creation itself: "God's glory is on tour in the skies, God-craft on exhibit across the horizon. Madame Day *holds classes every morning*, Professor Night *lectures each evening*. Their words aren't heard, their voices aren't recorded, but their silence fills the earth: *unspoken truth is spoken everywhere*" (Psalm 19:1–4 MSG, emphasis added).

In addition to creation, God teaches us through His written Word: "All Scripture is inspired by God and profitable for teaching, for reproof, for correction, for training in righteousness" (2 Timothy 3:16 NASB). And His Word (specifically the portion known as "the Law") was given for a purpose: "Therefore the Law has become our tutor to lead us to Christ, so that we may be justified by faith" (Galatians 3:24 NASB). Jesus was God in the flesh, and who could make God known more clearly than God speaking face-to-face?

"No one has seen God at any time; the only begotten God who is in the bosom of the Father, He has explained Him" (John 1:18 NASB). Peter understood this when he exclaimed, "Lord, to whom shall we go? You have words of eternal life" (John 6:68 NASB).

And as if Christ's earthly appearance wasn't enough, we are given the Spirit of God to be our Teacher forever! "'But the Helper, the Holy Spirit, whom the Father will send in My name, He will teach you all things, and bring to your remembrance all that I said to you'" (John 14:26 NASB).

Holy Teacher, You alone give light to our understanding. Help us to keep our eyes and our minds open to all that You have to teach us.

The Right Kind of Student

I will instruct you and teach you in the way which you should go; I will counsel you with My eye upon you. Do not be as the horse or as the mule which have no understanding, whose trappings include bit and bridle to hold them in check, otherwise they will not come near to you.
PSALM 32:8–9 NASB

• •

As a good Father, God provides opportunity after opportunity to learn—about Himself, about ourselves, about the world, and about eternity. He is a faithful Teacher and promises to "counsel" us as we apply His teaching to our daily lives.

As an involved, loving Teacher, what kind of student is God hoping for? What kind of student makes any teacher happy? What kind of child makes their Father's job a delight? Certainly not those who need to be guided like a senseless animal, pulled along day after day. Being resistant to learning is a grief to any teacher and useless to any student. "Obey your leaders and submit to them, for they keep watch over your souls as those who will give an account. Let them do this with joy and not with grief, for this would be unprofitable for you" (Hebrews 13:17 NASB).

The goal of all teaching is to pass along new information, resulting in a new perspective, which in turn leads to a new experience. In other words, growth. Our Mentor wants to see us imitating Christ, making our own choices, and taking risks. He wants us to grow up in our understanding and see the changes in us, just as any good dad, or coach, or counselor would.

Good Father, forgive my resistance to growing up! Help me to listen more attentively to Your teaching. I want to grow and to please You as my Father, just as my own kids delight me as they develop. Help me to focus on the things You value and stop wasting time seeking my own ways.

Seven Qualities of Spiritually Effective People

*Do your best to improve your faith. You can do this by adding
goodness, understanding, self-control, patience, devotion to God,
concern for others, and love. If you keep growing in this way,
it will show that what you know about our Lord Jesus Christ
has made your lives useful and meaningful.*
2 PETER 1:5–8 CEV

. . . .

Dads know a lot of things—at least our kids think so when they're young!
The fact is, most men enjoy being good at something, whether it's fixing
things around the house, developing a career, or pursuing a sport or a
hobby. We love the idea of being effective, of pursuing goals and achieving
results. It's in us by design. Being really outstanding at something means
acquiring a set of specific skills. Men spend a lot of energy acquiring the
right skills for the job.

But in spiritual work—in building the kingdom of God—skills are not
the main concern. Certainly they have their place, and God gives each
of us spiritual gifts to be used to help others grow (1 Corinthians 12:7).
But effectiveness in the kingdom is tied to the character of the worker.
Peter points us to seven "qualities" that make up a foundation for being
useful and fruitful in God's plan. The promise is pretty clear—we can't
fail if we possess these qualities as growing traits because "no grass will
grow under your feet, no day will pass without its reward as you mature
in your experience of our Master Jesus" (2 Peter 1:8 MSG).

While we grow in our abilities, talents, and gifts from the Lord, let us
remember Peter's admonition to be diligent in adding the qualities that
lay a true spiritual foundation for effectiveness.

*God my Father, You have allowed me to have life in
Your Son. Help me to become a man like Him: loving,
patient, devoted, good, and always relying on You.*

Happy Endings

*For I am confident of this very thing, that He who began a
good work in you will perfect it until the day of Christ Jesus.*
PHILIPPIANS 1:6 NASB

. . . .

To "perfect" something means to work on it until it's right. Another way
to translate "perfect" is to "carry it on to completion" (NIV). Christ does
not start something in us only to leave it all in our hands. God already
tried that, in a manner of speaking. The Old Testament Law was that very
opportunity, but it could not make us right with God (Romans 3:20), and
it had no power to make us different from the inside (Romans 8:3). It
takes Christ to do those two things. That's why Jesus is the "*author and
finisher* of our faith" (Hebrews 12:2 KJV, emphasis added). We begin a
journey with Christ, who not only promises to walk with us, but assures
us of a happy ending.

Our journey with Christ is part of a process called *sanctification*. The
part we experience in our daily lives is when we begin to think and choose
the way Jesus would—the way a son would—approving "the things that
are excellent, in order to be sincere and blameless until the day of Christ"
(Philippians 1:10 NASB). This is in stark contrast to the Law that didn't
require an internal change but still required blamelessness. The Law was a
long and burdensome road, traveled alone. But it was meant to be so we
would welcome the help of a Savior (Galatians 3:24). Now, since it's His
work in us and not our work for Him, we can have confidence for a lifetime.

*Thank You, heavenly Father, for not leaving us to our own efforts,
but giving us the promise of becoming a mature son by the help
of Jesus, our Savior. You are a good and loving Father.*

Godly Rebuke

And they came to Him and woke Him, saying, "Save us, Lord;
we are perishing!" He said to them, "Why are you afraid,
you men of little faith?" Then He got up and rebuked the
winds and the sea, and it became perfectly calm.
MATTHEW 8:25–26 NASB

• •

The disciples were an unlikely mix of educated and uneducated, craftsmen and professionals, strong character and weak. But nothing breaks down barriers like a life-threatening event. When the storm threatened to swamp their boat, the disciples were all in agreement: wake Jesus up!

Of course Jesus comes through for His fearful men, but the storm wasn't the only thing that got rebuked that day. He wasn't grumpy for being awakened; He was disappointed in their lack of faith. It's ironic to think that calling on Jesus for help could bring a rebuke. In this case, it would have shown more faith for the disciples not to cry out for Jesus' help. After all, He was right there with them.

Peter repeats this watery lesson later: "Peter got out of the boat, and walked on the water and came toward Jesus. But seeing the wind, he became frightened, and beginning to sink, he cried out, 'Lord, save me!' Immediately Jesus stretched out His hand and took hold of him, and said to him, 'You of little faith, why did you doubt?' " (Matthew 14:29–31 NASB).

As any father knows, there comes a time when holding your child's hand actually holds him back. Just as our kids need to grow and mature, so do we as disciples of Jesus.

The lesson they seem to keep reviewing is that fear is the most potent form of doubt. Jesus wants us to be free from fear and live like He is truly with us, even in the storm.

Good Father, help us to see You and to reckon on Your
presence in every trial and hardship. Help us to become
men of faith, trusting You through every storm.

Curses to Blessings

Shimei was yelling at David, "Get out of here, you murderer! You good-
for-nothing, the LORD is paying you back for killing so many in Saul's
family. You stole his kingdom, but now the LORD has given it to your son
Absalom. You're a murderer, and that's why you're in such big trouble!"
Abishai said, "Your Majesty, this man is as useless as a dead dog!
He shouldn't be allowed to curse you. Let me go over and chop off
his head." David replied. . . "If Shimei is cursing me because the
LORD has told him to, then who are you to tell him to stop?"
2 SAMUEL 16:7–10 CEV

• •

A child grows up learning to listen to the rebuke of his father and mother
and, hopefully, benefit from it! It takes humility, even as a toddler, to
change when someone else corrects you.

As a believer, we are asked to listen to God through His Word and
His Spirit and respond. That takes another degree of humility. But a
willingness to hear from God even when it comes from someone who
hates you—now that's a challenge!

King David was running for his life from his son Absalom who had
usurped his throne. Along the way, an embittered old man from Saul's
family took the opportunity to ridicule David. "Pay back!" shouted Shimei.
Of course he was wrong, but David did not even attempt to correct him.
He did not retaliate (though he could have) on the chance that God
was using this moment to speak to him. He simply trusted in the Lord's
judgment of the situation.

It's hard enough not to defend ourselves when confronted by a friend.
But what about someone who honestly doesn't care about us? When
we are rebuked, are we willing to look for God's message to us even in
the words of those who are ignorant and hurtful? God's voice would be
worth the effort.

Father, help me to be humble and to accept rebuke.

Being the Man

[King David to Solomon] "I am going the way of all the earth. Be strong, therefore, and show yourself a man. Keep the charge of the LORD your God, to walk in His ways, to keep His statutes, His commandments, His ordinances, and His testimonies, according to what is written in the Law of Moses, that you may succeed in all that you do and wherever you turn."
1 KINGS 2:2–3 NASB

• •

Solomon had the unique though difficult blessing of being at his father's side as he was dying. Few men get that kind of farewell, and fewer still get the life-directing exhortation that would guide Solomon as the next king of Israel.

David was a warrior and a successful king, leaving Solomon with huge boots to fill—a "man's man" as they say. But at the end of his life, what did he point to as the basis for being a man? Keeping "the charge of the LORD"—following wholeheartedly the ways God had revealed. And that, he well knew, would take courage. So David clarified things for Solomon so all the other issues he would potentially wrestle with in life as a man—purpose, success, legacy, leadership—would fall into place. David did not want Solomon to be distracted by what the world says a man is but to be a man in God's eyes first and foremost.

Solomon's defining moment had come, and with it the weight of a kingdom but also the blessing of being set on the right course. For all men, in all circumstances, being on the firm foundation of God's will makes a man succeed as a man.

O God, You alone are the Father that we need to please. We want to "show ourselves men" as we seek You and put You above every other blessing that can be found in this life. Give us each a heart to follow You without reserve and to pass that blessing on to our children.

Godly Hate

"If anyone comes to Me, and does not hate his own father
and mother and wife and children and brothers and sisters,
yes, and even his own life, he cannot be My disciple."
LUKE 14:26 NASB

• •

It's obvious that Jesus is not instructing us to actively hate our families. That would be absurd, since it would contradict just about everything else the Bible says is a man's responsibility to his family. Likewise, despising oneself is not the point since God loves us and has adopted us. *Contrast* is the point—Jesus is illustrating the impossibility of being a true disciple if there is competition for His supremacy.

In the verse, Jesus lists the most likely competitors for His rightful place in our hearts, our minds, and our choices. He doesn't list career or success. Those things can be serious distractions, but they aren't what truly compete for the affection of sincere believers. It's relationships that contend with Him the most—other personalities and desires. Other voices. Choosing a godly "hate" of family is an important philosophical position. It needs to be in place so that when following Christ means alienation from those closest to us, our love for Him is the *only* love that matters. He wins, hands down.

Then there's our own desires, our own voices. If we cling to our vision for ourselves, then that will disqualify us from being His disciple. If what we want matters more than growing in the true knowledge of the One who created us (Colossians 3:10), we won't be *able* to follow Christ. He's not the one who rejects our service—we make ourselves unavailable.

*You, and You alone, Almighty Father, deserve our devotion. There can
be no competition for our hearts, though we love our families and
would give our lives for them. Help us to always see eternity when
things begin to compete with You in our minds and hearts.*

Experiencing God, or the Other Way Around?

Work out your salvation with fear and trembling; for it is God who is at work in you, both to will and to work for His good pleasure.
PHILIPPIANS 2:12–13 NASB

• •

As a baby only knows his side of things, it's perfectly understandable that new Christians focus on their personal experience of God. It's okay because, like a baby, new believers bring joy and pleasure to their Father by simply existing. But as children grow in their understanding, they are expected to make their parents happy by showing maturity and character—to carry on the family name in an honorable way. Likewise, believers are born to please God by reflecting His divine nature.

Paul consistently connected knowing God with pleasing Him. He prayed that believers "may be filled with the knowledge of His will in all spiritual wisdom and understanding, so that you will walk in a manner worthy of the Lord, to please Him in all respects, bearing fruit in every good work and increasing in the knowledge of God" (Colossians 1:9–10 NASB). Our growing understanding of God gives us new experiences of Him, but it also gives God new experiences of us. As we mature spiritually, we gain the opportunity not just to receive from our Father, but to give to Him. And the great news is that not only can we bring our Father pleasure (1 Thessalonians 4:1), He Himself is so committed to His own experience of us that He actually works in us to see that it happens. If we want to make Him happy, we have nothing to stop us!

Good Father, You have blessed us with the opportunity to make You happy! What love You have for us! Thank You for making us into sons and giving us Your Holy Spirit to guide and strengthen us as we grow into pleasing sons.

Learning Wisdom and Self-Control

Proverbs will teach you wisdom and self-control and
how to understand sayings with deep meanings.
PROVERBS 1:2 CEV

• •

Self-control doesn't come naturally for most of us. Raising children shows us a clear picture of the problem we face for the rest of our lives. If you have given up hope and given yourself over to one sin or another, Solomon has something to say to you. In the verse above, he says the book of Proverbs will teach you wisdom and self-control. Hope does exist. You just have to access it.

When is the last time you worked your way through the book of Proverbs? There are thirty-one chapters in Proverbs, one for each day of the month. Would you be willing to spend some serious time and contemplation in one chapter of Proverbs per day for the next month? Would you be willing to journal about your revelations? How about enlisting another man to go through them with you? Commit to not talking about anything temporal during the month, but instead speak only about the truths you are learning. It might be awkward at first, but awkward is okay. All it will take is one revelation to set you on a new course.

Solomon says that in addition to gaining wisdom and self-control, you will learn how to understand sayings with deep meanings. This doesn't come as a natural gift, or even a developed skill. It comes from the Spirit of God as you ingest the wisdom of His Word.

If your soul has been dry during this season of sin, expect a change. Expect deep understanding. Expect deep revelation. Expect victory.

God of love, we need self-control to be able to walk with You
and not chase useless distractions. Strengthen us, make us wise,
and show us where we need to grow in self-control so we can
focus on Your kingdom and Your righteousness!

Pleasing the Weaker Brother

*If our faith is strong, we should be patient with the Lord's followers
whose faith is weak. We should try to please them instead of ourselves.*
ROMANS 15:1 CEV

• •

If you've ever wondered whether you fall into the "stronger" or "weaker"
brother camp as expressed in the scriptures, the truth in Romans 15:1
might help you answer that question.

Generally speaking, stronger brothers have been and continue to
be immersed in the Word. They have clarity regarding the precepts of
God. They are under authority and accountable. And they treat those
who are just starting out in their faith journey with the utmost respect
and patience—so much so that they try to please their brother rather
than themselves.

When it comes to matters of food and drink and various other issues
that fall under the banner of Christian liberty, stronger Christians should
never attempt to flaunt such liberties, but rather be sensitive toward
the weaker believer who is still formulating his personal theological
understanding of such things.

If that means not ordering a glass of wine at dinner with a weaker
brother who might object, then the stronger believer gladly does so
out of love and concern for how his actions might be perceived by the
weaker brother.

As the weaker brother grows, he will find himself in the presence of
newer, weaker brothers, and your witness of loving him right where he
was will help him to do the same for others.

*Father, just as we would never undermine our own children by putting a
stumbling block in front of them, help us to guard the souls of our weaker
brothers and sisters. Pour out Your great love in our hearts so that we
take care to restrict our own liberties willingly and without resentment.*

Put Off Anger, Put On Christ

Don't make friends with anyone who has a bad temper.
PROVERBS 22:24 CEV

• •

The biblical principle of not befriending people who have a bad temper is meant to keep us from becoming just like those people. We are influenced by the people we hang out with, and vice versa. That's why we don't want our kids "running with the wrong crowd." There's little room for grace in the life of a hot-tempered man, and wisdom is far from him.

But most of us know this. In fact, we nod our heads in agreement when we read this verse, believing it to be good common sense, but have you ever considered it from the opposite point of view? Are fellow believers avoiding friendship with you because you have a bad temper? If you know you have a problem with anger and are currently experiencing isolation as a result, now is the time to ask for help.

Approach your pastor, small group leader, or someone who has known you for a long time and allow him to ask you hard questions that examine your motivation. Once you find your triggers, you can begin the work of putting off your spirit of anger and putting on the mercy of Christ.

If anybody ever had a right to be angry, it was Jesus. He was betrayed, falsely accused of blasphemy, beaten beyond recognition, and executed in the most painful of ways. But after conquering death, He was anything but angry. Instead, He was with His apostles for forty more days, speaking about God's kingdom (Acts 1:3)—one that practices love, happiness, peacefulness, patience, kindness, goodness, faithfulness, gentleness, and self-control.

Patient and loving Father, help me to be at peace and to remember that man's anger does not bring about the righteous life You desire. Show me where my anger comes from so that, with the help of the Holy Spirit, I can put those issues under the lordship of Christ.

Become a God Pleaser

I am not trying to please people. I want to please God.
Do you think I am trying to please people? If I were
doing that, I would not be a servant of Christ.
GALATIANS 1:10 CEV

• •

The apostle Paul was indeed a people pleaser at one point in his life. As a Pharisee, he studied to show himself approved by men. As a persecutor of those who followed Jesus, he pleased men by holding the coats of the men who stoned Stephen to death (Acts 7:58). He even approached the high priest at one point for permission to persecute Christians (Acts 9:1–2).

Post conversion, Paul became a God pleaser, contending for the Gospel at all cost, no matter what man thought. His letter to the Galatian church was a warning. He heard that they were straying from God and ultimately the Gospel as it had been taught to them by the apostles. His language was sharp, saying, "I pray that God will punish anyone who preaches anything different from our message to you! It doesn't matter if that person is one of us or an angel from heaven" (Galatians 1:8 CEV).

As believers, we are called to love one another and our neighbors as ourselves in humility. And pleasing people is not always bad, as when a child works to please his parents. But when a false gospel is presented, we must speak the truth as lovingly as possible. We cannot afford to be people pleasers when it comes to the Gospel. Souls are at stake. We are not servants of Christ if we compromise in this area.

God, You alone offer the truth that can save the world—how can we
let people's opinions sway us from declaring that truth? But sometimes
we do! Convict our hearts of the importance of Your message so
that we never consider pulling back in the face of opposition.

A Leader of Honor

Every honest leader rules with help from me.
PROVERBS 8:16 CEV

· ·

In our modern world in which leaders often try to cover up one scandal or another, it's easy to lose trust in leaders of all stripes—from political to religious to business. But some leaders are indeed honest, and whether they know it or not, they are only able to be so because God governs the affairs of men at every level.

God cares about how our presidents, governors, senators, members of congress, and mayors use their power. He wants to see them use their power for good, not for personal gain. He cares about how pastors, elders, and Sunday school teachers shepherd the flock. He wants to see them use their power to bring His people to a deeper understanding of Him, which helps us draw closer to Him. He cares about how CEOs, COOs, CFOs, and the like run the companies they have been entrusted with. He wants them to use honest weights and measures because trusted companies lead to stable economies.

At some level, you are a leader. You are a leader at work, at church, or at home—maybe all three. Do those who are under your authority trust you? Would they say you are honest? If you have made mistakes or committed sins in your leadership role, ask for forgiveness. And then trust God to help you to be the honest leader He spoke about in Proverbs 8:16.

Father, Jesus was the most trustworthy leader the world has ever experienced. Make us more like Him when we lead in our families, our work, our church, and our community. Teach us to shepherd people and to sacrifice ourselves as Your Son did for us.

Reporting for Duty

But when the week was over, we started on our way again.
All the men, together with their wives and children, walked with us
from the town to the seashore. We knelt on the beach and prayed.
ACTS 21:5 CEV

• •

Pastors will tell you that men in America are largely AWOL in both attendance and in the work of the church. Women, on the other hand, are plentiful and willing subjects, anxious to be used by the Lord in any capacity He sees fit. But that's not the way it is supposed to be.

In Acts 21, Luke chronicles Paul's journey that ultimately led to Jerusalem, where he faced harsh persecution. When the ship he was on stopped in the port of Tyre in Syria for a week to unload its cargo (verse 4), the shipmates went in search of other believers. When they found them, they grew quite close—staying with them and listening to their warnings not to go to Jerusalem. Paul was undeterred, however, deciding to press on. But before he did, all of the men took their wives and children to the seashore to see him off. They kneeled and prayed.

Not a single member of this group of believers was AWOL. Every one of them accompanied Paul all the way to the seashore, and then they sank to their knees to implore heaven to keep him safe. Imagine the difference the modern church could make if every believing man reported for duty. If you've been AWOL, it's not too late to change that.

God, our Father, we want to step up to serve in Your kingdom!
We want to lead our families into that service as well. Where else
will our children learn the importance of working for eternal things?
Thank You for Your patience with us as we learn to sacrifice our
own plans to be part of something much, much greater.

Modeling Consistent Self-Control

Tell the older men to have self-control and to be serious and sensible.
Their faith, love, and patience must never fail.
TITUS 2:2 CEV

. . . .

The apostle Paul left Titus, one of his charges, behind in Crete to do the difficult work of appointing leaders for the churches in each town (Titus 1:5). Paul gave him instructions about which type of men to choose as leaders, as well as instructing him about the type of people they would be ministering to.

Paul quoted and confirmed what one of the Cretan prophets said, "The people of Crete always tell lies. They are greedy and lazy like wild animals" (Titus 1:12 CEV). He wanted Titus to be hard on such people so they could grow strong in their faith (Titus 1:13). This brings us to the verse above regarding older men in Crete. Ordinarily, older men don't need to be told to have self-control and to be serious and sensible, but apparently the older men in Crete were among those who were greedy and lazy and therefore needed to hear this message.

When young Christian men are unable to look up to older men in the faith in matters of appetite control, a sense of hopelessness can set in. If older Christian men cannot temper the flesh, what hope does a young man have? Regardless of where you find yourself on the age spectrum, self-control is not only possible, but followers of Christ are called to exhibit it.

Father, each one of us is an older man to someone! What a tremendous resource godly older men have been in my life—
help me to become that same encouragement to other men!

Starting at Home

Crispus was the leader of the meeting place. He and everyone in his family put their faith in the Lord. Many others in Corinth also heard the message, and all the people who had faith in the Lord were baptized.
ACTS 18:8 CEV

• •

Crispus was the ruler of the synagogue at the time Acts was written. As the ruler, he would have presided over the assemblies, interpreted the law of God, and judged whether actions were lawful or not, among other duties. As such, the Jews certainly wouldn't have expected to see a mass conversion to Christianity from his household, but that is exactly what happened.

Crispus is believed to have come to the faith either after hearing Paul's preaching or when he was in Justus's house. Either way, once he became a Christian, it changed everything. Under his leadership, Christianity spread even farther—that's the mark of a true Christian leader. His love for the Lord was contagious, and he couldn't wait to share it with everybody he loved, beginning in his own household.

In modern America, often mothers are the ones who pass along their faith to their children because men are busy with other pursuits. But nothing is more important to our children than good news of the Gospel. The children God has entrusted to us are our number one "mission field" so to speak. When will we ever have so much opportunity to influence anyone else in this world for Christ?

Father, You have made families the most important building block in human society. No wonder You love to see entire families come to the knowledge of salvation! Give us wisdom to share Christ in our own families in the midst of all the other complexities of family life and to be patient with children who may not yet believe.

Wall Building

Losing self-control leaves you as helpless as a city without a wall.
PROVERBS 25:28 CEV

• •

During biblical times, cities often had walls built all the way around the perimeter for protection from the outside. The walls also probably kept people on the inside from wandering into trouble on the outside. Smaller villages were often unwalled (Ezekiel 38:11; Leviticus 25:29–34) and, as a result, were easier prey for predators.

When we lose self-control, Solomon says we are as helpless as a city without a wall—open, vulnerable to attack, an easy mark for Satan. The converse is also true—a person who has self-control is as safe as a city with a wall. This analogy is hard for us to fully grasp today since none of our cities are walled and since we live and move among people who will gladly lead us far from the Lord. It might sound silly to try to re-create the notion of wall building for the purpose of maintaining self-control, but those who practice it will tell you it helps them stay on track one hour at a time.

The practice could be called building "hedges," and the process looks different depending on the person. It may take the form of an accountability partner or filters on a computer to keep our eyes from straying. Other issues may require a hedge of geography—you simply can't be in a bar, at a party, or near a particular set of old friends. Maybe you can't do the shopping anymore because all you buy is junk! In any case, we are all responsible to take steps to protect us from being defeated. Not just for our own sake, but for our families.

What sort of wall can you build to keep yourself and your family safer?

Holy Father, we know we are in this world but not of it—but we also have weaker areas than others. Some struggles we can't imagine and others we can't seem to resist! Help us to take the time to figure out how to build a wall, or hedge, of protection against those things that would ransack our lives.

Replacing Our Childish Ways

When we were children, we thought and reasoned as children do.
But when we grew up, we quit our childish ways.
1 CORINTHIANS 13:11 CEV

• •

A recent *Christianity Today* article makes this observation about the state of men: "Recently, several articles and statistics have shown that women are making history with career achievements, while men in increasing numbers are seemingly living in a prolonged state of adolescence, sitting back with their buddies and playing video games."

Throw in fantasy football, rampant use of pornography, and a growing disinterest in marriage, and you have a near epidemic of men who never grow up. Of course, video games and fantasy football, in moderation, are fine. But when they take the place of work, sacrifice, service, worship, and responsibility, they become sinful.

Our prolonged state of adolescence extends even to our faith. Some of us became Christians at an early age. We were baptized under the direction of our parents. We attended Sunday school. We read our Bibles. But then we graduated from high school, got a job, moved, and quickly fell away. As a result, some of us are in the same place spiritually that we were five, ten, and twenty years ago. What father would be okay with seeing his children stagnate like that?

Paul spoke of quitting childish ways in today's verse. What sort of childish activities are you engaged in that you need to put away? Replace them with spiritual activities and you'll begin to see spiritual growth that will help you make an impact for the kingdom.

Father, I want to grow up in Christ! Help me to acknowledge and give
up those selfish ways that hold me back from maturing in the Lord.
Teach me to say no to things that waste my time or compete with my
spiritual health. Thank You for being a committed, caring Father.

Knowing When to Hide

*When you see trouble coming, don't be stupid
and walk right into it—be smart and hide.*
PROVERBS 22:3 CEV

. . . .

As a dad, part of our job is to teach our kids when to stand up to something and when to protect themselves. Sometimes situations call for us to stand boldly against injustice or in favor of the oppressed. The prophet Nathan stood against King David and his sin of adultery (2 Samuel 12). Peter and John stood against Annas, Caiaphas, and other members of the high priest's family when they were told never to teach anything about the name of Jesus again (Acts 4).

Other times we are called to run and hide, as mentioned in the verse above. Several translations describe the person in this verse as "prudent." In other words, they are wise—immersed in the scriptures, able to know the difference between when to stand and when to run. And when trouble is on the way—the type of trouble that doesn't need to be confronted, they run. Noah heard God's voice, saw impending trouble, and he hid in the ark. Joseph was tempted by Potiphar's wife, and he ran in the opposite direction.

Do you see trouble coming in your own life? What is your first instinct? Whatever it is, how does it compare or contrast with the wisdom of the verse above? If you haven't fully developed your sense of discernment, consider enlisting the help of a godly friend who can help you navigate the situation, and maybe avoid one of the biggest mistakes of your life.

*Father, make us wise to know when to stand and when to be prudent
and avoid conflict. Teach us to hear Your voice in these things and to be
connected to You every day so that we are in step with Your Spirit.*

Heavenly Correction

Our earthly fathers correct us, and we still respect them. Isn't it even better to be given true life by letting our spiritual Father correct us?
HEBREWS 12:9 CEV

· ·

We tend to run at the first hint of correction. Correction is humiliating and pride crushing, even when it's justified. When you were growing up and faced the possibility of discipline because you did something wrong, you probably not only hid, but you also fretted, begged, and pleaded before finally submitting to your punishment. You may see it in your own kids.

But, assuming you weren't physically abused, when you were older you were thankful that your earthly father cared enough to correct you, because it made you the man you are today. You probably even respect your father for stepping in when the situation warranted it because now you can see the fruit.

The writer of Hebrews indicates that something much larger is at stake than simply becoming a better person. When we go astray spiritually, our heavenly Father has to step in because *true life* is at stake, meaning eternity in heaven.

Putting the theological debate about eternal security aside and just examining this verse for what it says, God loves us enough to correct us in such a fashion that will keep us from experiencing true death as the result of our wayward actions. If you are experiencing His correction or have done so recently, rejoice! You are being prepared for heaven by our Creator.

Good Father, thank You that You love us enough to correct us and make us more like Your Son! Help us to be patient in discipline, so that we benefit from it. Teach us to value Your correction over anything we would choose for ourselves.

Who, or What, Rules You?

People who are ruled by their desires think only of themselves.
Everyone who is ruled by the Holy Spirit thinks about spiritual things.
ROMANS 8:5 CEV

• •

I need coffee. Time for a shower. What should I wear? How am I doing on time? Why doesn't this guy in front of me drive any faster? I wonder how my 10:00 a.m. meeting will go. Who took my parking spot? Why is the receptionist so grumpy every morning? I hope I don't have any difficult problems to solve in my e-mail inbox this morning. I hope Greg doesn't stop by my desk for his typical twenty-minute chat. I have too much to do for that. The meeting went better than I thought it would. Hope the kids don't need help with their homework tonight. What's on TV?

If you were to keep a running list today of every major thought you have, what would it reveal? Would your typical day look anything like the paragraph above? None of these concerns are bad or even selfish, necessarily, but for a Christian to go an entire day without contemplating spiritual things is an indication of a spiritual problem because the Holy Spirit naturally directs and guides us as we go about our daily routines.

As we submit to Him, we see otherwise mundane tasks and situations through spiritual eyes—eyes that want to honor and obey God, eyes that earnestly desire to see beyond our own desires, eyes that want to minister to others. We are quicker to forgive and slower to anger. We long for heaven, rather than the recliner.

Father, help me to become a man who sees spiritually and takes action. Forgive my slowness to serve and my quickness to become wrapped up in myself. Help me to be a true servant even in the smallest things, and let it begin in my own house.

Knowing God

*Let's do our best to know the LORD. His coming is
as certain as the morning sun; he will refresh us
like rain renewing the earth in the springtime.*
HOSEA 6:3 CEV

• •

In Hosea 6, the prophet is addressing God's people after a period of sin, saying, "He has torn us to shreds, but he will bandage our wounds and make us well" (Hosea 6:1 CEV). After we have experienced His discipline, Hosea tells us to do our best to know the Lord. This will look different for everybody.

Some of us will turn to what saints of old referred to as the spiritual disciplines. Richard Foster listed twelve such disciplines in His classic, *Celebration of Discipline*: meditation, prayer, fasting, study, simplicity, solitude, submission, service, confession, guidance, celebration, and worship. Others of us find the disciplines to be too formulaic and opt instead for a freer form of expression, often focusing on one or more of the disciplines outlined by Foster.

Hosea didn't tell us to adhere to one expression or the other as much as he called us to perform some sort of action to know the Lord. You picked up a copy of this book because you want to know Christ in a deeper fashion. That is a great indicator that you are on the right path. What else are you doing to know the Lord? If your children came to you and asked how you draw closer to God, what would you say?

*Father, I want to know You and be filled with Your Holy Spirit. I want
to go deeper in my understanding and walk more closely with You.
Help me to take discipline as a blessing toward You and to pursue
You in the habits that godly men of the past have used so effectively.*

Jump-Start Your Prayer Life

In certain ways we are weak, but the Spirit is here to help us.
For example, when we don't know what to pray for,
the Spirit prays for us in ways that cannot be put into words.
ROMANS 8:26 CEV

· ·

As men, we often have a more difficult time expressing ourselves verbally than women do about things that matter. That doesn't mean we aren't emotional or passionate, and it certainly doesn't mean we don't need to feel a connection with other people; but when it comes to finding the right words to build relationships, they are hard to find.

In 2007, researchers from the University of Arizona conducted an eight-year study and determined that, contrary to popular opinion, men and women speak approximately the same amount of words each day: 16,000. It also found that men tended to talk more about technology and sports, while women talked more about relationships. In other words, men talk about things and what other people are doing, while women speak about how they connect with people.

Maybe this explains why so many Christian women are prayer warriors while Christian men are busy talking about theology. Since we struggle to express ourselves in relationship, we struggle to talk to God. We talk about Him, instead. But the Spirit is here to help us in our weakness, even going so far as to pray for us when we don't know what to say. That implies we are actually talking to God on some level. Where we fall short, the Spirit takes over. Find both comfort and motivation in that truth to jump-start your prayer life.

Good Father, thank You for the gift of Your Holy Spirit, who helps us in our weakness. Make us bolder to bring things to You in prayer and to daily lean on Your Spirit to strengthen us and guide us into all truth.

Heaven's Register

But don't be happy because evil spirits obey you.
Be happy that your names are written in heaven!
LUKE 10:20 CEV

• •

After Jesus sent out His seventy-two hand-chosen followers to every village and city He planned to visit, they returned to Him and said, "Lord, even the demons obeyed when we spoke in your name!" (Luke 10:17 CEV). Jesus acknowledged that fact, but He didn't want their focus to be on the power He had given them. Instead, He wanted it to be on eternity. Their names were written in heaven. That is something to be happy about.

Many of us spend our entire lives trying to get our names known in the business world, hoping to climb the ladder of success as our star rises. And to a degree, there's nothing wrong with this. But if our joy and our satisfaction comes from having our nameplate on an office door on the top floor of a tall office building, it will be short lived.

Being known as a good husband and father is nobler than career achievements, but even that identity can't be the truest source of our joy. The joy and satisfaction that does not fade and is not vulnerable to changing circumstances comes from the fact that our names are written in heaven!

In John's Revelation (21:27 CEV), he gets a peek inside the New Jerusalem, and he sees the book that will contain our names: "Nothing unworthy will be allowed to enter. No one who is dirty-minded or who tells lies will be there. Only those whose names are written in the Lamb's book of life will be in the city."

If you have been born again, rejoice that your name can be found in heaven's register this very moment.

Father, You have included us in the Book of Life through Your Son, Jesus. We praise You for eternal life—the greatest miracle of all!

Encourage One Another Daily

You must encourage one another each day. And you must keep on
while there is still a time that can be called "today." If you don't,
then sin may fool some of you and make you stubborn.
HEBREWS 3:13 CEV

• •

Motivational speaker Jim Rohn once said, "You are the average of the five people you spend the most time with." You can find a variation of that sentiment in 1 Corinthians 15:33 (NIV) when the apostle Paul quoted Greek poet Menander: "Do not be misled: 'Bad company corrupts good character.' " In a passive sense, we become the type of people we hang out with. This is why we dads want to know the kind of friends our kids make.

As Christians, we are called to be active in our pursuit of godliness. One of the ways we are to be active is to encourage one another each day. If we don't, sin will fool us, making us easy prey for Satan—much like the lone sheep is easy prey for the hungry wolf. Receiving such encouragement presupposes that we are active members in a congregation and that people there know us well enough to offer and receive encouragement from us.

If that's not the case for you, then find a good, Bible-believing church. Once you've found a place of worship, seek a kindred spirit or two and figure out the best way to encourage one another on a continual basis. Some Christian men exchange Bible verses via text message every day. Others meet for coffee a couple of times each week. And others sneak away during the lunch hour to pray for one another. Find what works for you, and devise a plan.

God of my life, I know I can't make it on my own. I need
brothers who will help me, correct me, watch out for me,
and always speak the truth. Bring me into that kind of fellowship.
Show me how to be that kind of brother to someone else.

Chasing Fantasies

Those who work their land will have abundant food,
but those who chase fantasies have no sense.
PROVERBS 12:11 NIV

• •

All of us have land to till each workday. It is our lot, and it has been assigned to us to provide for our families. For some, it is physical land; for others it is a real estate office, a teller window, a delivery truck, a taxicab, or an office. While our tasks may feel like drudgery at times, an attitude of diligence and gratitude can, and should, spur us on.

Just as farmers work in different stages—from cultivation, to preparing for the crop to come, to harvest—our jobs require constant preparation. It's a never-ending, time-consuming cycle. It doesn't have to come at the expense of time with our families, hobbies, or even starting a new business, though. When Solomon condemns fantasy chasing in the verse above, he's referring to sloth and inactivity—not hardworking entrepreneurs who are busy tilling new ground. In Adam Clarke's *Commentary on the Bible*, he says it this way: "He who, while he should be cultivating his ground, preparing for a future crop, or reaping his harvest, associates with fowlers, coursers of hares, hunters of foxes, or those engaged in any champaign amusements, is void of understanding."

Father, open our eyes to see where we are chasing fantasies at the expense of our real work. Give a combination of humility and wisdom so that we work with joy, knowing we are doing what You've called us to do.

God's Will

It is God's will that you should be sanctified: that you should avoid sexual immorality; that each of you should learn to control your own body in a way that is holy and honorable.
1 Thessalonians 4:3–4 niv

. . . .

The will of God isn't illusive or hidden. We are to give thanks in all circumstances, because this is the will of God for us in Christ Jesus (1 Thessalonians 5:18). It is God's will for us to perform good works so we can silence ignorant talk of foolish people (1 Peter 2:15). And it is God's will that we should be sanctified, or holy, avoiding sexual immorality.

Giving thanks, performing good works, and controlling our sexual urges are not mutually exclusive. When we are thankful and working out our salvation, our sexual urges are better kept in check. On the other hand, when we grumble about our circumstances and are idle and cut off from Christian community, our baser instincts demand attention. This is true inside of marriage as well as outside.

Giving thanks in all circumstances means we are willing to accept the truth of Psalm 16:5: the Lord is our portion; He makes our lot secure. We aren't owed anything more or less than what He has determined ahead of time, including sexual fulfillment. Submitting to this truth is part of the sanctification process.

Performing good works brings a sense of joy that replaces worldly happiness that comes from pleasing the flesh. And if you're married, the best place to start is with your wife!

Father, You created sexual desire and also the plan for it. But in our society we are bombarded with false promises and deceptive alternatives. Help us to fill our minds and our hearts with Your perspective as we serve others who are truly in need.

Hide the Word in Your Heart

I have hidden your word in my heart that I might not sin against you.
PSALM 119:11 NIV

. . . .

Raising children will teach you a lot about human nature. Kids hide things for two reasons. They are either ashamed of something or they treasure something so much that they have to hide it for fear that someone will steal it. We do the same things as adults.

David knew great sin, but he also knew great forgiveness. In his experience, hiding the Word of God in his heart was the only way to combat his sinful nature and to keep him from falling even further.

To say that he hid the Word in his heart implies several things. First, he went beyond simply owning a copy of God's Word. Owning a copy isn't transforming. Second, he went beyond hiding the Word in his mind. Our memories can fail us. Third, he went beyond simply reading God's Word on occasion. Reading it is helpful. But possessing it in our hearts is transformative.

If you find your faith lacking the power to overcome sin, consider a Bible memory program. It doesn't have to be elaborate. Index cards will work just fine. Look up verses that speak to the sin you are struggling with and jot the verses down on the cards. Carry them with you everywhere, and refer to them throughout the day.

If you meditate, study, and recite the verses often enough, you'll find that they are hidden in your heart—the perfect place for the Holy Spirit to access them for your spiritual breakthrough.

Eternal God, my Father, You have given me a written history of
Your great love and the ability to read—I am without excuse!
Help me to go even deeper than just reading, to mediating and
memorizing Your truth. Help me to hide Your treasures in my heart daily.

Putting on Christ

Let the Lord Jesus Christ be as near to you as the clothes you wear.
Then you won't try to satisfy your selfish desires.
ROMANS 13:14 CEV

• •

All of us go through spiritually dry seasons in our Christian walk. Our desire for Christ and His Word are lacking. Prayer is nonexistent. We have to make ourselves attend worship, or sometimes we even give in to the temptation to stay home. Spiritual truths are hard to digest. And circumstances don't make sense.

One day, our spiritual fog lifts in the form of a word that is aptly spoken in a song, in a book, from a child, or in a sermon and we realize that God was there all along. We were the ones who strayed, not Him. Even in the depths of our despair, we probably know this to be true, but knowing isn't enough. In the verse above, Paul tells us we need to let the Lord Jesus Christ be as near to us as the clothes we wear.

Think about that for a minute. The clothes you are wearing are touching your skin right now. They are tangible. You can feel them. Wherever you move, they go with you. You don't have to do anything to make them go with you, other than to move your body. In fact, you have to remove them intentionally to be free of them.

Can you point to a time in which you intentionally removed Jesus from your life, chasing after your sinful desires, as the verse above says? Is it possible that your spiritual dryness began that very day?

God, we long to be clothed in Christ! Help us to keep Him closer
than the clothes we wear. Forgive us when we lay Him aside to
pursue our own ways, as if we could just remove Him like a coat!
Father, help us to persevere in dry times, knowing You are always with us.

Sustaining Grace

*Let us then approach God's throne of grace with confidence, so that
we may receive mercy and find grace to help us in our time of need.*
HEBREWS 4:16 NIV

. . . .

Many of us live our entire lives in search of our father's approval. Inherent
in his perceived approval is a list of accomplishments he expects us to
complete. For some, it's a six-figure income, a seven-figure house, and a
beautiful wife. For the more spiritually minded, it could be an expectation
to become a pastor, a full-time missionary, or at *least* an elder or deacon.

The problem with all of these expectations is twofold. First, God
may not be in any of them. He may have something completely different
in mind for us. Second, once we get caught up in seeking our father's
approval at the expense of point number one, we end up playing a game
of merit. As long as we do what our earthly father wants us to do, we are
on track to gain his approval. But the moment we stumble, his approval
is withdrawn, and often we become a shell of what we could have been.

God, on the other hand, tells us to approach His throne of grace
with confidence. Notice that it is called a "throne of grace," not a throne
of rules we have to follow to earn His love or approval. As we approach
Him with confidence, we receive even more grace (rather than judgment),
and that grace sustains us in time of need.

*I rejoice in You, my Father and my God! You approve of me in Christ;
You call me "son" because of Christ; You have asked me to approach
You with confidence because of Christ. Help me to be that kind of
father to my own children, and that kind of man to the world.*

Becoming a Man of Noble Character

But the noble make noble plans, and by noble deeds they stand.
ISAIAH 32:8 NIV

. . . .

Would you consider yourself a man of noble character? If so, you're a man who knows God and His calling on your life. You're a man who is value and purpose driven. You're a man with a firm grasp of what's eternal. Sadly, this world is full of bored men, lazy husbands, and disinterested fathers.

The truth is, at times *every* man gets bored. Dr. Harold Dodds, then-president of Princeton University, made this counterintuitive observation: "It is not the fast tempo of modern life that kills but the boredom, a lack of strong interest and failure to grow that destroy. It is the feeling that nothing is worthwhile that makes men ill and unhappy." What captures your imagination? What fires your soul because it's worth your best efforts?

Finding our passion in God will come out in our daily choices. Things will change the more we embrace His plan for our lives. We will find ourselves saying no to some things. True, some of those other things may not *feel* boring, but they lack any connection to or passion for the Lord God, Creator of heaven and earth—and they lack any lasting honor, let alone value for eternity. The answer isn't to stop everything you're doing. Each established sphere of life is important to God. That includes your continuing education, vocation, marriage, family, church, neighborhood, community, and much more. How do you see God in each sphere? Conversely, how does God see you in each? This is the calling and the journey of a noble man.

Loving Father, I want to be noble in Your eyes! I want to have a passion for You and Your righteousness that puts everything else in its proper perspective. Help me to surrender my own ambitions and to become fully Yours, just as You fully offered Your Son in my place!

Working with All Your Heart

Whatever you do, work at it with all your heart, as working
for the Lord, not for human masters, since you know that
you will receive an inheritance from the Lord as a reward.
It is the Lord Christ you are serving.
COLOSSIANS 3:23–24 NIV

• •

How strange that the all-powerful, omniscient Lord God, Creator of heaven and earth, allows human hands and hearts to do His will. The man of noble character trusts God to work in and through him. Such a man doesn't waste his time longing for a life without God's calling and purpose. He certainly doesn't waste it longing for a life of excitement, dissipation, pleasure, and ease. A noble man is a God-filled, purpose-driven, and busy man. His hours and minutes are measured and meaningful. "Being busy is not a sin," Max Lucado wisely observes. "Jesus was busy. Paul was busy. Peter was busy. Nothing of significance is achieved without effort and hard work and weariness. That, in and of itself, is not a sin. But being busy in an endless pursuit of things that leave us empty and hollow and broken inside—that cannot be pleasing to God."

Looking back on the past month, what is your experience? To what degree were you busy with the right things—family, work, ministry. . .your own health? Are you working to see God's will in all areas of your life? Are you living intentionally? How we approach our daily calling, whether wholeheartedly or halfheartedly, makes all the difference in the world.

God, You weren't halfhearted when You gave Your Son for the
sins of the world. You take no delight in slack work or slack attitudes.
Help us to make our lives busy with the right kinds of things:
loving, serving, helping, sharing, witnessing.

Doing What Is Right No Matter What

[He] who sows to the Spirit will from the Spirit reap eternal life. Let us not lose heart in doing good, for in due time we will reap if we do not grow weary. So then, while we have opportunity, let us do good to all people, and especially to those who are of the household of the faith.
GALATIANS 6:8–10 NASB

• •

The noble man knows that he can achieve nothing if he doesn't love God with all his heart and love others as himself. He also knows he can achieve nothing without the Holy Spirit's daily cleansing, filling, and fruit-bearing work in his heart and life. Why is it so hard to live such a life? It's difficult, and often impossible, if you are unsure of the eternal value of your goals, if you are overwhelmed by the tasks before you, and if you doubt God's greatness, goodness, and calling on your life. It can be like kids going to school day after day not seeing the importance education has on the rest of their lives. It's critical, but it feels more like a burden when the alarm goes off!

Phillips Brooks is best known for authoring the Christmas carol "O Little Town of Bethlehem." He was also arguably one of the best known and loved American pastors during the latter part of the nineteenth century. He loved the Lord, studied the scriptures, proclaimed the Gospel, lectured and preached at Harvard, published a number of books, and helped create one of the nation's most magnificent church buildings. His clarion call still echoes after all this time. "Do not pray for easy lives, pray to be stronger men. Do not pray for tasks equal to your powers, pray for power equal to your tasks." As you put this book down, ask God to strengthen you today.

God of strength and hope, help us to realize the eternal value in what we do today. Show us how to serve You today. Help us to see Your kingdom even in the mundane things we will face today. Make our today Your today, O Lord!

Saying and Doing What the Lord Commands

*The days of our lives are seventy years; and if by reason of
strength they are eighty years, yet their boast is only labor
and sorrow; for it is soon cut off, and we fly away.*
PSALM 90:10 NKJV

• •

In addition to writing the first five books of the Hebrew scriptures, Moses also penned Psalm 90. This psalm appears to have been written between the events recorded in Exodus chapters 2 and 3. The pleas in verse 13 and other verses certainly seem to point to a period before the call of Moses. And the lament of verse 10 seems to correspond with Moses' age at that time. Of course, little did Moses know what God had in store for him over the next forty years! In those "extra" four decades, Moses was more alive on so many levels than during the previous eighty years. What made the difference? Moses was saying and doing what the Lord commanded.

The noble man does the same. He wants to live a full life infused with God. Then again, he is ready to face death at a moment's notice. In his advance directive for end-of-life care, a man added a brief letter addressed to his wife and oldest daughter. In it he said, "I have enjoyed life more than most. I have the sure hope of heaven when I die. I may die later today or fifty years from now. When I'm near the end, I fully trust whatever decisions you make. Please never forget how much I love you." May we be able to say the same.

*Father of life, You have given us a time on this earth to seek You and to
serve in Your kingdom. As men, as husbands, as fathers, as workers,
help us to know You more and to share You in word and deed.*

Embracing the Enormity of God's Calling

So teach us to number our days, that we may gain a heart of wisdom.
PSALM 90:12 NKJV

. . . .

Few men know which decade, year, month, or day they will die. Then again, at the very end of his life, Moses knew which day he would die. The same can be said for only a small handful of biblical characters. Yet knowing the day of one's death isn't necessarily good news. Like most people, Moses wanted to live longer. If anyone had good reason, he did. After all, Moses longed to enter the promised land and enjoy the "milk and honey" awhile.

Yet God alone appoints the day of one's death. Not even the best of men is exempt. So, it's imperative that we aspire to live nobly before God, our families, and others *now*, not someday. We may not have tomorrow to be the man God wants us to be today. "Today" is much more closely connected to eternity than tomorrow—tomorrow is an idea; today is a reality.

The purposes of God are bigger than we can imagine. That's why eternity always must be in view. A. W. Tozer said it well: "Life is a short and fevered rehearsal for a concert we cannot stay to give. Just when we appear to have attained some proficiency we are forced to lay our instruments down. There is simply not time enough to think, to become, to perform what the constitution of our natures indicates we are capable of." Only by embracing the eternality of God's calling can we face death with nobility.

Eternal God, our Father, open our eyes to this day, to this moment.
Teach us to use it for Your glory. Show us eternity in each
opportunity we have to serve You, our families, and others.

Asking God for Even More Courage

"The thief comes only to steal and kill and destroy;
I came that they may have life, and have it abundantly."
JOHN 10:10 NASB

. . . .

Life is full of circumstances that test our courage. Winston Churchill once said, "Without courage, all other virtues lose their meaning." It doesn't matter that you're honest, for instance, if you're afraid to tell the truth. Or that you're responsible if you're afraid to try anything new. It's ironic that our society is bent on the idea of trying to become more rebellious, more risk taking, less inhibited, more outrageous, less self-controlled. Many blame these trends on the 1960s, but the reality is—people have always been bent away from self-control.

This bent against self-control, however, inevitably hurts our community, our families, and our friends. Ultimately, it hurts us. If you and I lack self-control, who's in control of our thoughts, speech, and actions? One option is we're giving in to the desires of the nature we were born with. That nature's passions and desires are anything but positive, healthy, or life giving. Another option is we may be manipulated or controlled by the Devil. If we let Satan control us, he will rob us of everything that's good in our lives. He will tempt us to take risky, dangerous, physically destructive, or suicidal actions that could kill us. So what other option is there? It's the option Jesus calls having "life. . .abundantly." Whatever you do today, choose that option! Specifically, ask God to strengthen you in your inner man, to cleanse and fill you, to cause you to be more self-controlled and courageous than ever.

Father, help me to understand the freedom that comes with self-control.
As a father, help me to bless my family by living an abundant
life in Christ and showing them His love in action.

Remembering God's Answers to Prayer

Though I walk in the midst of trouble, you preserve my life.
You stretch out your hand against the anger of my foes;
with your right hand you save me.
PSALM 138:7 NIV

• •

In his book *Stories of Faith and Courage from the Korean War*, retired Marine Corps Lt. Col. Larkin Spivey tells the story of Pvt. Ed Reeves. "LORD, if the mortar didn't kill me, the shooting didn't kill me, and the beating didn't kill me, you must want me out of here. But I can't walk. How can I get outta here?" As Reeves lay helpless on the frozen ground beside the now-abandoned and destroyed truck convoy, he continued to pray. Suddenly, God seemed to answer: "You must crawl before you can walk." Painfully lifting himself to his hands and wounded knees, Reeves started crawling over snow-covered fields in the direction he hoped would take him to friendly lines.

He passed more Chinese troops who somehow made no effort to stop him. Darkness fell, and he continued his slow, painful journey. He began to sing over and over, "Yes, Jesus loves me!" Finally, he felt the hardness of ice underneath him and knew that he was on the Chosin Reservoir.

Exhaustion and the mind-numbing cold were almost overwhelming day after day. Amazingly, the song of his childhood faith kept coming back to him: "Jesus loves me, this I know, for the Bible tells me so." Finally, almost a week after being first wounded, Ed Reeves was rescued. One of his first comments? "Every time I asked God, He answered."

Good Father, You answer Your children when we call out!
Maybe all we can muster is a song or a single verse to offer You,
but You are with us in all we endure. Strengthen our faith so that we
do not take hardship for abandonment, or suffering for a lack of care.

The Most Important Thing about You

"You are worthy, O Lord, to receive glory and honor and power;
for You created all things, and by Your will they exist and were created."
REVELATION 4:11 NKJV

• •

What is the most important thing about you? Who you are? Your family name? What you've done? What you plan to do in the future? What your children will say about you when you're gone?

Actually, none of these take top priority. Instead, the most important thing about you is your view of God. A. W. Tozer put it this way: "Without doubt, the mightiest thought the mind can entertain is the thought of God, and the weightiest word in any language is its word for God." He goes on to say: "The most portentous fact about any man is not what he at a given time may say or do, but what he in his deep heart conceives God to be like. We tend by a secret law of the soul to move toward our mental image of God." Sadly, the images of God prevalent today are "so decadent as to be utterly beneath the dignity of the Most High God and actually to constitute for professed believers something amounting to a moral calamity."

If you say you believe God can do anything but expect Him to do nothing, is it any wonder you find it hard to pray? Conversely, if you thank God daily for His greatness and goodness, His holiness and love, and His mystery, is it any surprise you like to talk about Him with others? So, what's your view of God today?

O God, my Father, open my eyes to know You as You really are! Destroy my vain speculations, refresh me with Your truth, and topple the image I have created of You in my ignorance. Transform me by Your Word.

Realizing God Is Greater Than We Can Imagine

Oh, how great are God's riches and wisdom and knowledge!
How impossible it is for us to understand his decisions and
his ways! For who can know the LORD's thoughts?
Who knows enough to give him advice?
ROMANS 11:33–34 NLT

• •

Every kid thinks their dad is the biggest, strongest, wisest man on earth. It's natural and healthy and sets the stage for understanding how much greater our heavenly Father is.

So, how big is God? What does it mean that He is the Creator and Sustainer of humanity, of Earth, of the solar system, of the Milky Way galaxy, of the universe? It means that the Lord God is infinitely bigger than human brains and minds can comprehend this side of heaven. So the foundation of any truths you might state about God is that you don't fully know what He is like. Mere mortals cannot grasp the attributes we ascribe to God, let alone comprehend the total character of God. So many aspects of His nature are mystery to finite man. The thesis of any discussion about theology proper, that is, the study of God, is that He is clothed in both majesty and mystery.

Walter A. Henrichsen is right on the mark when he says, "Every problem a person has is related to his concept of God. If you have a big God, you have small problems. If you have a small God, you have big problems." So, how big are your problems? You may be struggling with wrong desires, gripping fears, critical health issues, financial problems, employment stressors, marital strains, parental pains, church issues, few meaningful friendships. Whatever your struggles might be, how big is your God? *How* big? Big enough, to be sure!

God, You are eternal and without equal. We are only a vapor that
appears for a short time without You! Nothing is outside of Your reach,
and Your love is more vast than all of creation. Open our hearts to
see that all we face in life is a small problem compared to You!

Remembering Why We Need God

*Your life is a journey you must travel with a deep consciousness of God.
It cost God plenty to get you out of that dead-end, empty-headed
life you grew up in. He paid with Christ's sacred blood.*

1 PETER 1:18–19 MSG

• •

Scores of times the Bible speaks about emptiness. *Void. Nothing.
Nothingness. Empty. Empty head. Empty-headed. Empty life. Empty-
hearted life. Empty hearts. Empty heart. Soul-empty.*

How empty? In *Confessions* Saint Augustine wrote: "Our hearts are
restless until they rest in You." Although Blaise Pascal didn't exactly coin
the phrase "God-shaped vacuum," he talked about it extensively. In
Pensées, Pascal said: "What else does this craving, and this helplessness,
proclaim but that there was once in man a true happiness, of which all
that now remains is the empty print and trace? This he tries in vain to
fill with everything around him, seeking in things that are not there the
help he cannot find in those that are, though none can help, since this
infinite abyss can be filled only with an infinite and immutable object; in
other words by God himself."

C. S. Lewis wrote a great deal about this need as well. He had started
his academic and publishing career as an atheist and agnostic, only to be
powerfully converted. In *Mere Christianity*, Lewis wrote: "If I find in myself
a desire for something which nothing in this world can satisfy, the most
probable explanation is that I was made for another world."

What is the longing of *your* heart? Family? Health? Security? All good
things have their place, but we were made to be complete only in God.
Ask God to fill every longing—with Himself—so you can enjoy life, and
enjoy it abundantly (John 10:10).

*Father, we thank You for offering us fulfillment in Your Son. You have
made us for Yourself, though we often try to fill the void with other
things, even good things, to no avail. Show us where we are allowing
our restlessness to drive us toward other things rather than Christ.*

Wanting God's Best for You

*I, Paul, am on special assignment for Christ, carrying out God's plan
laid out in the Message of Life by Jesus. I write this to you, Timothy,
the son I love so much. All the best from our God and Christ be yours!*
2 TIMOTHY 1:1–2 MSG

• •

What does it mean to want and receive God's best for you?

First, it means discarding inadequate, insufficient, ignoble thoughts of God. Any son who misunderstands his father is destined to miss opportunities to please him. Herman Melville said, "The reason the mass of men fear God, and at bottom dislike Him, is because they rather distrust His heart, and fancy Him all brain like a watch."

Second, wanting God's best means seeing Him as He really is. David Needham writes, "I am convinced that the answers to every problem and issue of life for both time and eternity are resolved through a correct understanding of God."

Third, receiving God's best means shedding your intense desire for temporal pursuits and possessions. George MacDonald observed, "Man finds it hard to get what he wants, because he does not want the best; God finds it hard to give, because He would give the best, and man will not take it."

Fourth, wanting and receiving God's best means desiring His will over and against your own will. C. S. Lewis put it this way: "There are two kinds of people: those who say to God, 'Thy will be done,' and those to whom God says, 'All right, then, have it your way.'"

What did you hope to gain this year? Have you gained it yet? If yes, is it God's best? If no, again, is it God's best?

*Good Father, I want Your best for my life. I want to please You by
living as Christ would. Help me to see You as You really are,
put aside anything that keeps me from walking with Your
Holy Spirit, and always put my will in submission to Yours.*

Childlike Faith

They entered the house and saw the child with his mother,
Mary, and they bowed down and worshiped him.
MATTHEW 2:11 NLT

• •

Are you wondering what to buy your loved ones for Christmas? Here's a bigger concern: Why is it so easy for many Americans to stop believing in Jesus when they "grow up" and "outgrow" the true meaning of Christmas?

It's deeply concerning how aggressively some ridicule the idea of childlike faith. Then again, it's worth thinking about what it must have been like for Jesus two thousand years ago. In complete contrast to the Messianic expectations of the ancient Jewish people, Jesus Christ didn't come out of nowhere riding into Jerusalem as a conquering hero. Instead, He entered this world in a most unexpected way: as an infant child. Have you ever thought about what Jesus did the first ten or twelve years after His birth? That's right: He was a boy. Why in the world would Jesus, God's Son, Creator of the heavens and earth, want to be a kid all those years? Wasn't that a waste of time? No. Absolutely not. First, it was fun being a kid! Jesus got to play with other children. Have you ever noticed that grown-ups sometimes worry too much and don't have enough fun? In contrast, Jesus invented a special plan so that, even though He was God, He could be a kid.

Ultimately, of course, Jesus became a child for a much bigger purpose. He entered this world as a child so that you could become like a little child and enter His world. *That* is worth pondering anew today.

Father, it's so good to be called Your child! Help us to appreciate
that blessing and to rejoice in the childlike faith that pleases You!
We thank You that we were born into Your family through
Jesus and can live a life pleasing to You!

Loving Jesus the Childlike Way

Continue in what you have learned and have become convinced of,
because you know those from whom you learned it, and how from
infancy you have known the Holy Scriptures, which are able to
make you wise for salvation through faith in Christ Jesus.
2 TIMOTHY 3:14–15 NIV

• •

Have you ever noticed that some grown-ups love to be around kids, and some don't? Even as a grown-up, Jesus loved to be with children. During His three and a half years of ministry as an adult, Jesus gives an amazing amount of priority to ministry to children. Jesus talks with children, something only parents and grandparents usually did in that culture.

Jesus commends the faith of little children, who in that culture were sometimes considered unable to truly embrace religious faith until they were almost teenagers. Not only that, but we see Jesus blessing children. We see Him feeding them. We even see Jesus using a little boy's sack lunch to feed the multitudes and send twelve hefty baskets full of leftovers to help feed others. Beyond that, we see Jesus healing boys and girls who are demon possessed and curing others who are sick and dying. He even resurrects a twelve-year-old girl who had just died and an older boy who had died a few hours earlier.

In His preaching and teaching, Jesus said that children are a strategic, essential part of His kingdom in heaven and on earth. In so many words, Jesus told His disciples, "Listen! My kingdom belongs to kids!" What's your own view of children and childlike faith?

You, O Lord, are the perfect Father. Help us to be good children! Show
us Yourself, and do not let our own worries and imagination keep us
from trusting You as a child should trust his Father. Make Yourself know
to us, and grant us the faith of a child to appreciate You more every day.

Zechariah's Surprise

"Do not be afraid, Zechariah, for your prayer has been heard,
and your wife Elizabeth will bear you a son, and you shall call his name
John. . . . And he will turn many of the children of Israel to the Lord
their God, and he will go before him in the spirit and power of Elijah, to
turn the hearts of the fathers to the children, and the disobedient to the
wisdom of the just, to make ready for the Lord a people prepared."
LUKE 1:13, 16–17 ESV

• •

Here we find Zechariah going about his business as a priest, working in an honored position and burning incense before the Lord. Suddenly an angel appears to him—Gabriel, one who "stand[s] in the presence of God" (Luke 1:19 ESV)—telling him that his wife, Elizabeth, in her old age would have a son, John, who would prepare the way for the Messiah. A repeat of Abraham and Sarah (Genesis 17:19–21).

Note what a part of John's task would be: calling Israel back to God, but also turning "the hearts of the fathers to the children." This echoes the last words of the Old Testament: "'Behold, I will send you Elijah the prophet before the great and awesome day of the LORD comes. And he will turn the hearts of fathers to their children and the hearts of children to their fathers, lest I come and strike the land with a decree of utter destruction'" (Malachi 4:5–6 ESV).

As a father, reread that passage from Malachi again. Notice that it doesn't talk about mothers here. Have you "turned your heart" toward your children, so that they turn their hearts toward you? Dads are the initiators in the family, setting the spiritual tone for better or worse.

Good Father, set our hearts right to seek You and to care for our
families as You care for us. Show us how to serve our children so they
are encouraged in their faith and honor You as their eternal Dad.

Gabriel Comes to Mary

In the sixth month of Elizabeth's pregnancy, God sent the angel
Gabriel to Nazareth, a town in Galilee. . . . The angel went to her and
said, "Greetings, you who are highly favored! The Lord is with you."
Mary was greatly troubled at his words and wondered what kind of
greeting this might be. But the angel said to her, "Do not be afraid,
Mary; you have found favor with God."
LUKE 1:26, 28–30 NIV

• •

The angel Gabriel once again gets called up for duty, just a few months
after he had appeared to Zechariah. This time, he appears to Mary, who
would become the mother of Jesus. As far as we know, Mary was an
unknown, normal teenager, perhaps fourteen or fifteen years of age. And
the angel came to her as she was in her daily routine—suddenly before
her stood a heavenly messenger with a shocking, even overwhelming,
task for her to accomplish.

Notice his words to her. He called her "highly favored" and told
her not to be afraid. Gabriel says these words of comfort, because his
appearance must have scared the living daylights out of her. (Angels
are always telling people not to be afraid, because they are awesome!)

We, too, are "favored" by God because of the saving work of Jesus
on our behalf. God has called us to live and work to build His kingdom,
and this passage calls us to fearless service.

Was Mary intimidated? Certainly. But her parents had instilled
something in her that was able to step up when the time came and
rejoice in God's calling on her life.

Prepare us, O God, for Your service! Help us, in turn, to prepare
the hearts of our children to embrace Your calling and Your work.
Help us to set an example of a ready heart and a humble spirit,
no matter what You ask of us.

Go Deeper into the Bible with These Resources